CONTENTS

Letters To A Software Practitioner:
Essays on Rejuvenating the Craft

Copyright © 2021 by Akram Ahmad.

FOREWORD

Why This Book? Why Now?

My conviction in the timeless beauty of prose and—just as importantly—its nexus with the rejuvenating qualities of beautiful code has grown stronger as the years have passed.

Having made such a bold statement, an explanation is in order: You must be wondering, after all, what this book is all about.

This is how it came to take shape, this is really how it happened, and this is why I am sending you, dear Reader—software practitioner or otherwise—a series of letters that make up the bulk of this book: I want to share everything I've learned about the beauty of the nexus between code—aka *"computer programs"*—and prose. (I have gone out of my way to make this book equally accessible to geeks and non-geeks; hence, my allusion a second ago to you, dear Reader, being a *"software practitioner or otherwise."*)

Here's the deal: Over the past two decades, the more code I've written up—and I can't help but think to the memorable phrase that "*I write code to understand better what I design*"—the more I've seen thrown into sharp relief a feedback loop at play, an ineffable loop that has the two (code and prose) informing each other in a virtuous cycle, with sometimes the *code* leading the charge and at other times the *prose*.

Put another way, the act of creating computer programs is, first and foremost, an act of *creation*. If this not be creativity, then I don't know what is. Enter prose, which is, to my mind, the flip side of the coin: As a writer, I sit down and engage in a creative act, one that's every bit as creative as its counterpart in the digital realm.

With that, I invite you to place your trust in me by giving me the privilege of serving as your guide: We are going to explore the underreported, symbiotic relationship between code and prose.

Where We Went Last Time

You may have read my previous two books—*Dispatches from the Software Trenches* and *Postcards from the Software Island*—the ones adorned by an admittedly longwinded *Foreword* each. I feel compelled to keep *this Foreword* far briefer, making the assumption that you've already got to know me a bit through the previous books' *Foreword* each. (You *have* read those two books?)

Then again, should this be your *introduction* to my written work, allow me to orient you. But first, an oh-so-quick interlude to gratefully acknowledge…

Your Warm Encouragement

I continue to be gratified by your rave reviews for my earlier books, for example these by readers just like you:

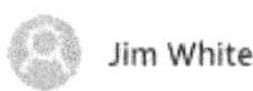 Jim White

⭐⭐⭐⭐☆ **Not a typical sofware engineering book**
Reviewed in the United States on March 8, 2021
Verified Purchase

This is a book for software engineers – but not in the way you might think. One does not read Akram's blog site or this book in order to learn about a specific programming language or software engineering skill. You are going to learn a lot about programming and engineering – and about the people that do this type of work – but this is not a how-to book. For those in the software engineering business, it's a professional repose. Best consumed on quiet nights with a brandy and contemplating your path through some of the same or similar "trenches" that Akram has traversed.
Akram's essays are a work of written and visual art. He is a story teller – he takes rather mundane software engineering topics and ideas and weaves them into Plato-styled dialogue and thought-provoking discussion. Some of the topics may be or may not be germane to your work as a software engineer. It won't matter. Enjoy the discussion if not the destination. At the very least, Akram provides you a profession reading list that will last you a career.

 Saqib Riaz Qazi

⭐⭐⭐⭐⭐ **In the age of information overload, Akram's unique writing style is a refreshing change!**
Reviewed in the United States on February 16, 2021

Akram always has something to say that gets you thinking, his distinct, genial and conversational approach is endearing and engaging. If anyone has truly experienced the "trenches" starting from the early days of programming the Z80 based ZX Spectrum in Basic and Assembly, its Akram! A book worth reading...

 TechEsq

⭐⭐⭐⭐⭐ **comprehensive , entertaining and passionate view of software development**
Reviewed in the United States on March 1, 2021
Verified Purchase

This easy read is a comprehensive , entertaining and passionate view of software development. Akram seemingly has a insatiable appetite for all things technical. Moreover ,he blends in analogies and tidbits from all of his other literary interests spanning philosophy, music and new wave media. This book is the proper next step from his blog: Programming Digressions which is a nice place to check in on current events in the space.
That said, this book is especially great for someone entering the world of programming. In my opinion that should be most of the population as we move forward in this fourth industrial revolution.

How We Got Here

So this whole writing business—using the word "business" in an enterprise sense—began with a blog I created earlier this century, right around 2014. The blog had a singular goal: Create reading material that I couldn't find elsewhere, material that I wished to read, except that nobody else had written it. So I went ahead and wrote it up myself. That's how you—and I—got the *ProgrammingDigressions* blog.

The fact that a ton of people—about 120,000 at my *original* blog and about 40,000 and-counting-and-losing-track-of at my <u>current</u> blog site—have made time out of their precious schedules to read what I write, I can only conclude that the blog has done well. *Really* well.

On Naming This Book

If the titles of my previous two book—*Dispatches from the Software Trenches* and *Postcards from the Software Island*—conjure up images of a roving imagination, you are right on the mark. To keep the traveling metaphor going, I reckoned that a series of letters (presumably sent from a journeyman) would be the thing to do. And thus do I trace the name of this book: *Letters to a Software Practitioner*.

Let's Open The Letters...

I hope you'll find enjoyment in reading these decidedly personal letters; writing them up sure kept me riveted!

Oh, I now begin to wonder, will these letters get delivered to you by the prim staff at the dainty post office in the quaint British town of Candleford—of TV series *Lark Rise to Candleford* fame —or perhaps our letter courier service will turn out to be the stealthy owls from the *Harry Potter* movies? *This* I know: These letters were written up just for you, straight up from an in-the-trenches software practitioner.

With that, let's start opening the mailbox and see what mail awaits us, by way of an oh-so-brief tick-tock TOC (Table Of Contents), like so...

Brief Table of Contents

Here's the proverbial 150,000-feet-view of what awaits you in the pages which follow. Here, then, are the marquee names of the eight "letters"—the eight essays—coming your way:

Letter I: *Why I Write*

Letter II: *How I Write*

Letter III: *Wow, I Write*

Letter IV: *Now I Write*

Letter V: *A Row With How I Write*

Letter VI: *Stellar Sentences Get Gangsta Treatment*

Letter VII: *Yer Edinburgh Ode to Microservices*

Letter VIII: *Beautiful Code, Beautiful Prose*

Rest assured that there is no vicarious or ethereal quality attendant on your reading these letters; they were *meant* for you to read, and in a tantalizingly tactile way at that.

With that, I make an exit so that, from here on, you can read the letters undisturbed. (As parting advice, I take the liberty of slipping in edgewise a word of caution: Keep your letters close to your chest, lest anyone have designs on them and seek to purloin them, macabre mystery maven Edgar Allan Poe—and his raven foe—notwithstanding, of course.)

LETTER I: WHY I WRITE

Writing a book is a horrible, exhausting struggle, like a long bout of some painful illness. One would never undertake such a thing if one were not driven on by some demon whom one can neither resist nor understand. For all one knows that demon is simply the same instinct that makes a baby squall for attention. And yet it is also true that one can write nothing readable unless one constantly struggles to efface one's own personality. Good prose is like a windowpane.

- George Orwell, in "Why I Write" (England Your England and Other Essays)

Dear Reader,

Have you ever had this feeling that *"writing a book is a horrible, exhausting struggle, ... [and how] one would never undertake such a thing if one were not driven on by some demon whom one can neither resist nor understand"*? If so, please know that you're in good company; great company, in fact, if you will glance at the name of author whose quote gingerly sits atop this letter.

Confession time: So I had similar doubts about the nature of writing, and not so long ago either. To that end—to find why you and I are in good company as I have claimed—let's listen to a dialog under way.

0. Readers Become Writers. Honest.

"Now tell me this, Akram, why in the world would anyone in their right mind want to listen to what you have to say on the fine art of writing? I mean, you don't teach writing at a university or something! So tell me what got into you that you decided to pontificate on why you write?"

Wasn't it taxing enough for legions of hapless readers who continued to suffer, even as they trudged through the desolate wilderness of your essays, that you've now taken it upon yourself to, um, *enlighten* them on the bleak—and oblique—considerations of *why* you write essays? I mean, *sheesh*.

We need to get your blog overhauled, not to mention this letter-writing which you've grown rather enamored of lately, what with your having gotten marooned on the fabled software island recently. We need to get that all overhauled; better still, *hauled* out of our sight this moment, towed away at the owner's expense, too: *yours*!"

Questions, Deep In Your Eyes

If those questions and thoughts—or a variant thereof—were welling up in your mind, let me assure you that those *very* questions and thoughts would've arisen in *my* mind had I contemplated writing this essay as recently as a year ago. But that was then, and this is now. Today, I'm not *so* sure where I stand on this matter
So what's going on? Let's give this a good look, shall we?

1. A-Hunting We Will Go

Before we get to the essay proper, here in a nutshell are the themes we'll be hunting for as this essay runs its course.
In other words, I will try to fish out—that is, out of the writer's swamp that is my cranium—the major reasons for *why* I write. Those themes will be the following:

1. Share my Expertise as a Software Practitioner
2. Help Clarify my Own Thinking
3. A Source of Inspiration
4. A Source of Joy
5. Accelerates Learning New Things
6. Boosts Relearning Things Anew
7. Aids in Learning Things Deeply
8. I Cannot *Not* Write

With those eight themes in mind, let's make a run…

What a piece of work is a man, how noble in reason, how infinite in faculties, in form and moving how express and admirable, in action how like an angel, in apprehension how like a god.
- William Shakespeare

2. The Essay, Reloaded

How The Essay Got "Written"

Oh, the outlandish analogies that your blogger has a penchant for cooking up, a' la *"The Essay Reloaded"*, and other stuff like that. So with profuse apologies to fellow fans of the amazing trilogy of movies that wowed us and which got their start in *The Matrix*—the original, dystopian movie—I sure wasn't beating around the bush when I said that the essay will be reloaded. So I had initially "written" this essay in my head during a three-hour drive back home to Austin—I was recently traveling back to my home after visiting Mom in Houston. Well, with the essay still floating around in the nooks and crannies of my cranium, several days had gone by.

Floating In Ether (Or Some Similar Medium)

And I *still* needed to "write" it down. I mean, an essay suspended in your blogger's cranium wouldn't have been of much use to you all, right, notwithstanding how the *Harry Potter* movies portray the utterly naive idea of "extracting" memories—funneling memories *out* of people's head and then, sheesh, pouring their glowing essence *into* test tubes—which seems even *more* far-fetched than the outlandish stuff that your blogger cooks up here in the *Programming Digressions* cafeteria (aka blog) on a routine basis?

First Would Come The Essay

Anyhow, as I sat down to write down my "virtual" essay—transfer it from its residency in my head to a slightly more indelible medium such as this blog—it dawned on me that actually not one but *two* separate essays were crying to be brought into existence, with this being the first of the two.

And there you have it. Many of you at this point will quite possibly be wanting to tell your blogger in no uncertain terms: "Hey, since you've already made us suffer through the dreary details of *why* it is that you write, you might as well put us out of our misery by *regaling* us—yeah, right, as if we really *mean* that—with the inglorious details of *how* you write your blithering tirades, and which you delude yourself about as somehow being essays proper."

To which I'll say: Hey, hey, *hey*—Let's all of us take a big, deep breath now, and let's do it *real* slow.

And Then Would Come The Sequel

The sequel—or prequel, or *something*—to this letter will be coming to a theater near you, so please stay tuned

Alas, the sequel won't be anywhere near as flamboyant as a marquee since I'm merely a lowly blogger on a shoestring blogging budget, writing for free. Nonetheless, we'll do another essay—to follow up on the one you're reading, "*On Writing: Or Why I Write*"—and which will be entitled something like "*On Writing: Or How I Write*".

Yep, the *How* is just as important as the *Why*. After all, without the *Why*, the need for *How* will simply not arise; if you don't have something to write about in the first place, it doesn't really matter whether you know the craft of writing backward and forward.

And without the *How*, the wherewithal to bring the fruits of *Why* would not be there; you may well have what you think is the most exciting thing you want to tell the world, but if you haven't mastered the modicum of the craft of writing, then is anyone going to even read your exciting essay? That to me is the stark reality.

On Disentanglement

At the same time—to add to a subtle twist to the considerations above—I recommend that you also keep in mind how infuriatingly hard it can be at times to disentangle the *Why* from the *How*, especially when it comes to matters as subjective as writing down the bones.

So I had wanted to tell you that there's this book—bones and all—which I discovered *literally* during the past 24 hours. *Truly great stuff though it is*—I found its honest and unapologetic wisdom speaking to my writerly self—it will have to wait for its day in the sun.

Onward.

Related Musings In An Earlier Essay

What I Had Said Then

It was, in fact, in an earlier essay that I had first shared some thoughts on *what* it is that compels me to write. There, setting the scene, I had remarked about how: First, and this is for the know-it-all *right* there in that back row, so he can't admonish me by saying, Hey

That's not writing, that's typing

Second, I generally avoid putting together (technical) tutorials, incredibly helpful as they are, simply because the internet is already awash with them; my inclination is to dig deeper, and share my findings with you, remaining mindful of the advice that

> *Originality does not consist in saying what no one has ever said before, but in saying exactly what you think yourself.*

Third, I strive to stay true to the gentle guidance—at once comforting and inspiring—in these memorable words which gently remind us that

> *True Ease in Writing comes from Art, not Chance,*
> *As those move easiest who have learn'd to dance*
> *- Alexander Pope (Sound and Sense)*

Fourth, and finally, I find myself resonating with this quote from George Orwell, though with *nowhere* near the acuteness which Orwell surely experienced when he divulged in "Why I Write" (*England Your England and Other Essays*) how

> *Writing a book is a horrible, exhausting struggle, like a long bout of some painful illness. One would never undertake such a thing if one were not driven on by some demon whom one can neither resist nor understand.*

Finally, I had mentioned, too, in that earlier essay: Okay, I feel much better already, having put it out there, as to exactly *why* I write; after all, should we all not start from the premise that "If you wish to converse with me, define your terms"?

And What I Say Now

What you got above are essentially some of my *earlier* musing in connection with exactly what it is that compels me to write. Today, I will elaborate a bit on all that—along with some allied undercurrents—so as to give you a fuller picture.

Here, then are the major reasons why I write. They are not necessarily in any particular order; they appear here simply in the order in which they popped into my head. Moreover, don't expect a masters class here. What I've got for you here are a handful of pointers.

This is very much *food* for thought, nothing less, and nothing more. Think of this as grist for the mill, which surely came from the grain that had soaked-in all the rain that falls mainly on the plains in Spain, or maybe even that lighthouse-decked island ahoy...

Knowledge of what is does not open the door directly to what should be.
- Albert Einstein

3. Point #1: Share My Expertise As A Software Practitioner

The desire to share my expertise as a software practitioner was instrumental in getting me started with writing—for my blog *ProgrammingDigressions* anyway. And the best way to illustrate what I mean by that (i.e. "sharing my expertise as a software practitioner") is, dare I say, by way of some examples of essays where I've attempted to do *exactly* that:

- The Fascinating World of Reactive Programming
- Blending Two Paradigms: Object Orientation and Functional Programming
- The Joy of Algorithms
- The Nuts and Bolts of Programming in Scala
- The Big Data Universe
- The Ins and Outs of Distributed Computing

Plese feel free to visit those essays, and by all means to explore any and *all* other essays (on the *ProgrammingDigressions* blog) as may grab your attention: Let me assure you that I'll be the *last* one to stand in the wayward ways of your errant explorations.

4. Point #2: Helps Clarify My Own Thinking

Readers will see the tell-tale compression of the pages before them, that we are all hastening together to perfect felicity.
—Jane Austen, Northanger Abbey

That writing helps clarify my own thinking has been a recurring theme for me lately. As they say, *"the best way to learn is to teach"*; and what better way to teach than to *write* about it?
And there you have it, the gestalt of how writing can help clarify one's thinking.

Nothing can cure the soul but the senses, just as nothing can cure the senses but the soul.
- Oscar Wilde

5. Point #3: A Source of Inspiration

Most folks I know look for inspiration to get *started* with writing. I'm the opposite: I start *writing* to get inspiration—In other words, what you've got here in your author is something of a paradox; the act of writing, for me anyway, is a *source* of inspiration.

Go figure.

The Unvarnished Truth

Please forgive me if what I'm about to say comes across as conceit or, worse still, as self-admiration, because nothing could be farther from the truth: The fact of the matter is that when I start writing, more often than not the sentences come out fully formed—all I have to do is type up those sentences, dress them up a bit, and that's *pretty* much it.

I hasten to add that the whole process isn't *exactly* like that—otherwise, writing would cease to be challenging and I would move on to something else—but that's as close to the unvarnished truth as I can put it. And I wouldn't lie to you, would I *ever*?

Pure (And High Octane) Inspiration

Speaking of inspiration, there's something you ought to know: My intellectual life can neatly be neatly divided into two halves. The first half was the one that that came *before* I discovered—and serendipitously at that, while browsing through our local brick-and-mortar Barnes & Noble bookstore—a gem of a book entitled *Plato and the Nerd*. The second half of my intellectual life is the one that has commenced *after* that discovery. It's no accident that I've devoted an unprecedented three essays

—yes, *three* whopping essays which can be found on my blog *Pro-grammingDigressions*—to a book that has become a part of me in a way that informs the very core of what it means to be a writer.

Plato and the Nerd has made for itself a place in my mind—nay, in my *heart*—that I could never have imagined giving to anyone, let alone to a *book*.

But then again, *Plato and the Nerd* is not merely a *book*. It's a call to a *revolution* in the way we—as humans—can go about imagining how best to conceive a creative partnership with technology; it's a call to a *revolution* of the most egalitarian kind imaginable, one that is suffused with thoughtful humanism.

Oh, The Headiness

I haven't seen the likes of it in my life: *Plato and the Nerd* has been tying up for me *so* many loose threads and themes—at *so* many levels at the same time—that I'm still reeling from the heady ex-perience of reading it for the first time.

Having shared the vignette above, I can only *hope* that it served to illustrate what I had in mind when I said that "*writing is a source of inspiration*", and on *both* ends, too: The *receiving* end (where I enjoy reading the works of fellow writers) and the *giv-ing* end (where I enjoy the unfettered act of engaging in writing down the bones).

Sprinting (Or, Maybe, Clambering Up The Roller-Coaster)

And please pardon my slight disorientation in what I've said above; it can be a roller-coaster ride at times.

Come to think of it now, here's an idea: I really can't do much better than refer you to what I've *already* written on my blog, *ProgrammingDigressions*—and *thus* far anyway—about my inspirational experience of reading the book that we just been chatted about, *Plato and the Nerd*:

1. Read up at your leisure the very first deep dive into its wherewithal and gestalt

2. Follow up that deep dive with a slightly different perspective on its offerings

3. Finally, settle down for a relaxed home stretch that's suffused with some slight poignancy

Best of all, *Plato and the Nerd* is written by a fellow nerd. He's one of *us* and not one of *those*

If *this* not be inspiration, I simply don't know what else it *could* be: Enough said about inspiration?

6. Point #4: A Source of Joy

Wrinkles should merely indicate where smiles have been.
- Mark Twain

Smiles all around when it's time to write: I can unequivocally repeat, "Yes, *sheer* unalloyed joy".

Right behind being a fertile source of inspiration, writing just happens to bring me great joy. It's a kind of joy that is unlike any other I've ever known. Imagine yourself as a kid having fun in your neighborhood playground—*that's* what writing means to me.

Speaking of writing and of playfulness, allow me to paraphrase Lord Chesterfield in noting that

Men and women are but children of a larger growth.

I also have to add—and this is the proud feminist part of me speaking here—that Lord Chesterfield had it wrong in what *he* had originally said, and part of which I just paraphrased above. He had it *totally* wrong when he had asserted that

Women are only children of a larger growth. A man of sense only trifles with them, plays with them, humours and flatters them, as he does with a sprightly and forward child; but he neither consults them about, nor trusts them with, serious matters.
- Lord Chesterfield

I mean, that is just *blatantly* wrong, what he said above. Wrong. Simply untenable. *Grrr...*

Okay, so I'm going to let bygones *be* bygones, but for crying out loud—and merely to take a theme or two as counter-examples—some of the best software developers I've had the privilege of working with are *women*. Some of the most thoughtful, capable, refined, and "strong" individuals—in every sense of "the latter quality" as I've come to understand it over the years—that I've had the pleasure of knowing have been *women*.

So there. *You* take that, Lord Chesterfield.

But I digress.

Plus, I'm not sure what *else* I could add to this particular point —that writing is a source of sheer joy—without belaboring it and perhaps even *diluting* its impact and effectiveness; we will, therefore, let matters "rest as they stand."

Hmm... Did I actually catch myself in saying above about how they may "*...rest as they stand*", did I now? That sounds a tad paradoxical, and for all I know, it just might drag us all down the rabbit hole of fathoming how fish are ever able to sleep. I mean, what *exactly* goes on? Do fish stand—or float, or hover, or remain suspended in semi-frozen animation—when catching their zzz's? These are the things I want to know, though *you* necessarily may not.

Okay, okay. Lest your writer—and you all in his wake—get dragged down the proverbial rabbit hole, let's scurry on to the next item.

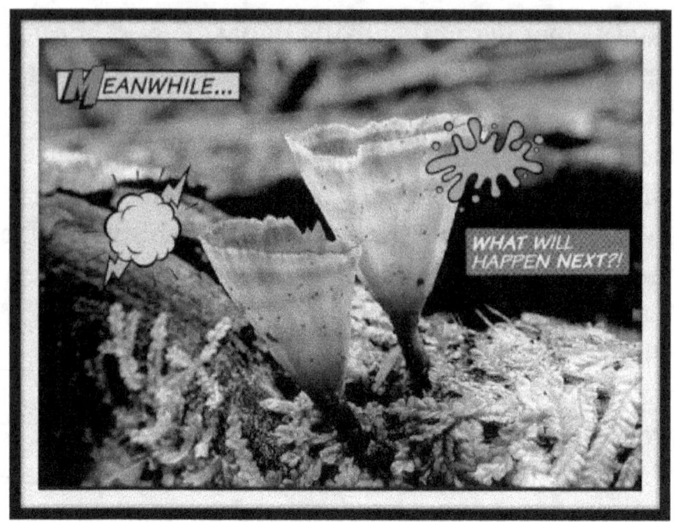

Read not to contradict and confute, nor to believe and take for granted... but to weigh and consider.
- Francis Bacon

7. Point #5: Accelerates Learning New Things

It's been said that the very best way to learn is to teach. So whenever I set my mind to learning—and mastering—a complex body of knowledge, I more often than not simply start writing about it, along with, of course, the obligatory doodling and stuff. And goodness, the things you'll learn in the process: For example, how little one *really* knows.

It's always a good thing, dare I add, to have a good laugh at oneself from time to time. But I digress.

On a slightly more serious note, there's nothing *quite* like writing to galvanize your learning process. Yes, I concede that there *are* all these other helpful accessories—mind maps, books-on-tape, *YouTube* videos, podcasts, Khan Academy, and so on and so forth. But if you want to truly master new things—and do so rapidly—there's nothing quite like *writing* about those things. And *while* you're doing your writing, make sure to also have some fun with doodling and stuff; engage *all* the senses at your disposal.

So it's not for naught whereby a wise adage uses the following words—and I feel these words paint an unmistakably evocative picture of a message—telling us that if you

> *Tell me, and I'll forget; show me, and I may remember; in-volve me, and I'll understand.*
> *- Chinese Proverb*

Enough said, methinks, so I won't belabor this point. Let's not tarry our sojourn much longer, lest anyone feels emboldened enough to accuse us of malingering. Oward.

> *Style is the substance of the subject called unceasingly to the surface.*
> *- Victor Hugo*

8. Point #6: Boosts Relearning
Things Anew

Anytime you wish to relearn something anew, I thoroughly recommend giving writing a try. It'll help you gain new perspectives as you could not have imagined possible.

Do please keep revisiting the basics, too. And that's a whole new topic right there.

Imagine beholding a dandelion in the beauty with which it offers itself—its heart wide open, knowing that it doesn't have much longer to live—doing so in a bold display of its near-kaleidoscopic, breathtaking existence, fleeting as its very existence is, at the mercy of the elemental wind which can snuff its life in the flash of an eye.

And *that* is what it means to *"relearn things anew."*

Should we be lucky enough, and I hope we *all* will be, to find that special book or two that spark our imagination—<u>*I sure found mine*</u> in the gem of a book that is *Plato And The Nerd* (The MIT Press)—then it's off to the proverbial races, with your mental accelerators wired to the floor.

You may also wish to peruse a related idea which would have us be mindful of how

> *He who studies books alone will know how things ought to*
> *be, and he who studies men will know how they are.*
> *- Charles Caleb Colton*

The idea above is one that I had elaborated on a bit as part of the vignette of David Perkins—in an essay on ProgrammingDigressions entitled Top Thought Leaders to Follow—who is with the Harvard Graduate School of Education, investigating human symbolic capacities and their development.

The aim of art is to represent not the outward appearance of things, but their inward significance.
- Aristotle

9. Point #7: Aids In Learning Things Deeply

Look, I'm an engineer and a computer scientist—all rolled into one—who has been practicing the fine art of programming for over two decades. The fact remains, though, that we *all* periodically need to deepen our understanding—and thereby our enjoyment—of the fine craft of programming. Yeah, it's a circuswheel all right; *loads* of fun.

We had other choices, yet we felt compelled to seek out this craft that literally takes years to master. No doubt this applies, to one degree or another, to any disciplines worth its salt. I'll go out on a limb and say, though, that the fields of engineering and computer science require a relentless commitment to learning that is unmatched by *any* other discipline.

And here I'll take the liberty of paraphrasing—in the most liberal way imaginable—the famous dictum of Thomas Jefferson when he opined that

The price of liberty is eternal vigilance.

What I propose here, in turn, as an analog to the Jefferson quote above, is that

> *The price of deepening your understanding is eternal learning.*

Now try *that* on for size.
And remember to learn on your own time, *not* on the time of your employer.
Remember, too, that it never hurts to stay fresh and mindful of the basics. And here I find comfort in the wise words of *William Blake* that

> *The true method of knowledge is experiment.*

The secrets of the complex and of the unknown lie, dare I say, in the simple and the familiar.

My own brain is to me the most unaccountable of ma-

chinery - always buzzing, humming, soaring roaring div-
ing, and then buried in mud. And why? What's this pas-
sion for?
- Virginia Woolf

10. Point #8: I Cannot Not Write

This one is going to be the hardest one to explain, which may explain why I (subconsciously) chose to save it for the end; then again, we save the best for last, don't we?

This one is straight from the heart. So even if it makes *no* sense at first, please bear with me.

The fact of the matter is—there are no two ways about it—that I simply cannot *not* write. For as long as I can remember, I've been... Writing. *And* reading: Swimming in a world of books and words, buoyed by the vistas which they kept opening up for me, allowing me to revel in the occasional rainbow or two, too.

While this point—that I cannot *not* write—may be a nebulous one, it's one that also happens to be *the* proverbial ticket to a life of writing.

11. Postscript

What Gives?

I could write more—a *whole* lot more—though I suspect we've suffered enough already. *"You took the words out of our mouth there, Akram"*, is in fact what I heard one misguided soul say, as if to affirm my own self-sentencing.

Anyhow, I was startled even as the waves of satisfaction washed down the deepest recesses of my soul. Have you ever had that feeling? The feeling when people and themes enter your life— the whole thing unfolding effortlessly like an emergent butter- fly unfolding its slender wings to mark its entry into the world —with it all happening so flawlessly that you find yourself trying to catch your breath. You stop.

And here I do *not* digress—which is a first here from our reading community of readers who flock to the *ProgrammingDigressions* blog—so please listen to the rest of the story.

You feel something in your throat as you try to fathom what's happening. You sense something tugging at your heart, but you can't put your finger on it. As a writer, these are the things I want to know.

And The Journey Began

So my journey had begun. And as they say, "the rest is history"— if there be mountains in our way, so much the better, to make the journey and the quest even *more* satisfying.

At this point, I'm sure that many—*all*?—of you are wondering: "Akram, aren't we *already* done with your essay?" Give me the pleasure, then, of informing you that, indeed, we are done with the essay.

But as we part—and until we meet next, there's something I wanted to say...

This Nearly Got Lost In The Shuffle

How could I have forgotten this delightful quote; reconnecting with it was like rediscovering a lost friend:

> *My method is to take the utmost trouble to find the right thing to say, and then to say it with the utmost levity*
> *- George Bernard Shaw*

I vividly recalled doing a double-take on first coming across these words: The sentiment enshrined in them have informed the *heart* of my writing ever since, *subliminally* for sure. Yet, I had somehow managed to forget them. *"Slap on the wrist, Akram, right now."*
Ouch, *that* hurt.

Rolling With The Punches

Take some comfort in knowing that the stuff I write is decidedly along the lines, too, of what the smart cookie Samuel Johnson—ace lexicographer from yesteryear—had in mind in remarking how

> *Your manuscript is both good and original; but the part that is good is not original, and the part that is original is not good.*
> *- Dr. Samuel Johnson*

Ouch, *again.*
But that's okay; I roll with the punches. I *had* to learn how to roll with the punches to survive, given that my birthday happens to be—yes, I kid you not—on *Halloween*. That's another, *long* story. And I do believe that you—dear Reader—have suffered enough already in trudging to the end of this letter. But hey, yay, the end is finally in sight.

Those Whale-Like Paragraphs

To wrap up, remember that nobody likes being greeted by—or being sunk under the oppressive weight of—whale-like paragraphs. Aim, then, to sidestep interminably long paragraphs, whenever temptation arises: Tellingly, master writers invariably use medium-length paragraphs; exceptions do exist, but know what you're getting yourself—and, in turn, your reader—into.

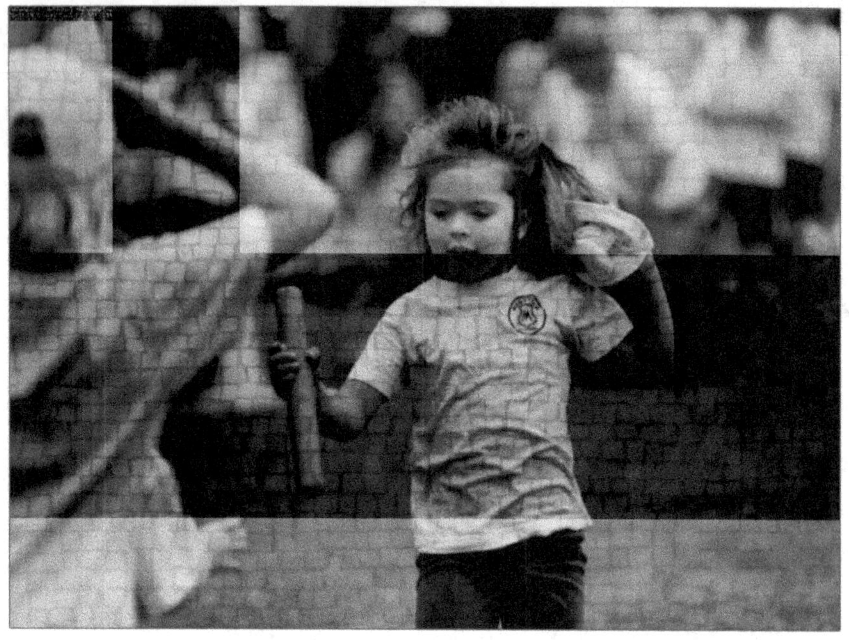

Explaining Metaphysics to the nation–
I wish he would explain his Explanation
- Lord Byron (Don Juan: Dedication)

That Oh-So-Elusive Goldilocks Writing Style

Another recurring theme that also informs the core of my writing came up, interestingly enough, when I was chatting with two dear friends just the other day. I was telling them about how they *both* have the knack for writing "Goldilocks" messages: Neither too long nor too short; instead, *just* right.

Sad to say, I'm simply devoid of that talent—I have only one style of writing: the longwinded one. (Talk about a single-track mind.) And you all are like, "*Akram, I mean, we are painfully aware of that.*"

Ouch. *Triple* ouch, now.

Back To The Basics

Maybe we'll revisit precisely this point; why, indeed, it makes sense to circle back to the basics; and of course my beloved onion metaphor. While you may not concur, the fact remains that themes do recur, and they do so big time. It's ritornellos all the way down.

So anyhow, as I sat down to write down my "virtual" essay—transfer it from its residency in my head to a more permanent medium—it dawned on me that actually not one but *two* separate essays were crying to be written.

Many of you at this point will quite possibly be wanting to tell your blogger: Hey, since you've already made us suffer through the dreary details of *why* it is that you write, you might as well put us out of our misery by regaling us—yeah, right, we mean that—with the inglorious details of *how* you write your ignominiously blithering harangues.

To which I'll say: "*Let's all take a big, deep breath right now.*"

Surely, You're Joking

The sequel, or prequel if you will, coming to a theater near you—relax, it won't be anything that flamboyant as a marquee since I'm merely a lowly blogger on a shoestring blogging budget who writes for free. So that sequel, or prequel or whatever, will be entitled something like: "*On Writing: Or How I Write*"

Yep, it sure is hard to disentangle the why from the how when it comes to matters as subjective as writing down the bones.

Oh, did I mention how—if you want to write well—you have to *read* a lot?

"Some people never learn! Hey, Akram, I thought we had suffered enough already, hadn't we?", you say. Indeed, you have—and to stave off the specter of yet another *"Ouch"*, an unprecedented ouch. Quadruple ouch—let's all of us pretend that I didn't even say anything about *reading* a lot.

Hmm... So You Weren't Joking

Should anyone wish otherwise, though, I'm going to talk about *precisely* that theme—the requirement that you need to *read* a lot if you wish to write well—as well as a bunch of other themes in the next essay, which I'm tentatively calling *"On Writing: Or How I Write."*

Meanwhile, I'm licking a postage stamp so I can slap it on the postcard and get it on its way to your doorsteps. And with that important message, I invite you to check the billowing clouds descend on the outskirts of Stevenson's fabled *Land of Counter-pane...*

I was the giant great and still

That sits upon the pillow-hill
And sees before him, dale and plain,
The pleasant land of counterpane
- Robert Louis Stevenson

◆ ◆ ◆

LETTER II: HOW I WRITE

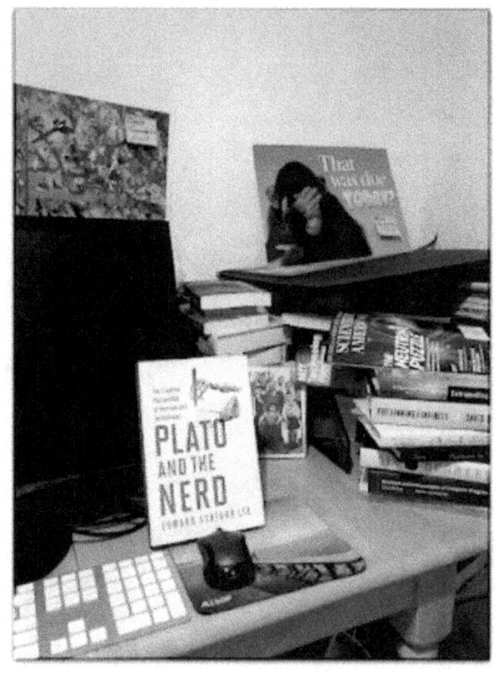

My method is to take the utmost trouble to find the right thing to say, and then to say it with the utmost levity.
- George Bernard Shaw

Dear Reader,

Back in the days when I was wont to watch Sci Fi thrillers, I was especially fond of the *Terminator* movie series. Now, before you run away aghast, wondering what such drama —gratuitously mayhem-laden that it patently is—might *possibly* have to do with the fine art of writing code and writing prose, let me hasten to add that those movies had *some* literary value, one easily susceptible to loss in the fray, especially given that its wherewithal lurks *well* below the layers of the movies' spectacular special-effects and non-stop drama engulfing the consciousness of viewers just like me (and you, too.)

To get a better sense for what I have in mind, let's roll the tape...

> *I'll be back*
> *- Terminator (the classic Arnold Schwarzenegger movie from which comes the immortal catchphrase above, one that will forever remain associated with Ahnold)*

As we near the scene, a feisty dialog is taking place—one between the writer and his esteemed readers—and we think twice about how to proceed. We finally decide, gulp, to jump into the fray...

Reader: *"Oh. My. God."*

Reader: *"He. Is. Back."*

Reader: *"He's actually doing it: We thought Akram was only joking when he had said in the previous essay—yeah, you know the one, that trashy, obtuse, blithering mess of an essay called "On Writing: Or Why I Write"—that he would be back with a follow-up essay. He was blabbering and prophesying then that it would be called "On Writing: Or How I Write", or something like that."*

Reader: "My, Oh My. Where does he get these outlandish ideas, if someone could only tell me that."

Reader: "Guess what? Looks like he's got another blithering piece here that is, eerily enough—someone pinch me if this is a nightmare —called On Writing: Or How I Write"... Insert a primal scream here.

Reader: "Oh. My. God."

Reader: "Some people just never learn, do they ever? I mean, despite all the feedback we gave him to cease and desist from further pontifications, Akram has the gall to return with yet another essay. Please put us out of our misery, and do it quickly!"

Reader: "That Akram guy sure can be a fast one; keep an eye on him before he gets it into his head to, heaven-forbid, terrify us by sending even bleaker essays our way. I mean, if you look at his pic here on the blog—you know, the one right above the gibberish where he says something like 'Hi there! I'm a Senior Software Developer...' or some-thing—you would think that he's the decent sort of person. Only now we know better."

Reader: "My, oh my! Looks sure can be deceiving: I mean, how can anyone be trusted when they don't hold back from writing back-to-back pieces of trash, his so-called 'essays' which are really thinly-disguised foolish talk that's been dressed up as highfalutin advice on writing. Worst of all, he's not even qualified to do any of this prat-tling; we have always known, after all, that doling out advice such as that is reserved for genteel critics, not riff raff like this blogger."

Reader: "And yet, here he is, barging into territory that's none of his business. Look, it's plain and simple: He ain't got no credentials—I mean, for crying out loud, does he teach writing or something at one of those fabled, online, phoenix-like universities?"

Reader: "Sigh."

Reader: "Get us through this, and please do it quick! Taking a deep breath before I dive. Counting to 100 now: 1, 2, 3, ... Someone? Any-one?"

Blogger: "And I says to you all—Whoah, gentle readers that thou all surely art, lend me thine ears, and your credit cards, too, should you wish, though the latter is not strictly required. Just kidding, just kid-ding; sometimes it's hard to resist a sophomoric joke or two."

Blogger: *"Ah, the irresistible pull of humor; imagining stuff like what happens when an irresistible force encounters an immovable object, and stuff like that. Cool, cool, eh."*

Blogger: *"Please listen to my plaintive diatribe—forgiving me my discursive style for a few moments—and I'll prove that I offer something of value. Obviously, your time is far more precious than mine—otherwise you would have done the writing part, and I would be doing the reading—plus you have my word that I'll treat your precious time with utmost respect; as for you credit cards, should you choose to lend them to me—in addition to your delicate ears—then all bets are off."*

Blogger: *"Do please listen to me for just a bit, and everything will be clear like mud. Oops, what I meant to say there was that everything will be oh-so-clear like the light of day in which we all can bask."*

Blogger: *"And yes, never again will the need arise to have talk of getting these essays hauled out of your sight. You know, towed away at the owner's expense, too; like, mine!"*

Blogger: *"If those questions and thoughts—or a variant thereof—are swirling around in your dusty cranium, I mean in the lovely antechamber of your magnificent mind, let me assure you that those very questions and thoughts would've arisen in my mind had I considered writing this (follow up) essay even as recently as a year ago."*

Blogger: *"But that was then, and this is now. Today, I'm not so sure where I stand on the matter of whether anyone should listen to my writing advice."*

How I Write: Advice From Your Resident Impresario

Let's put some things on the table before we read another word:
As I sat down to write this up, I did not consult any resources—online, or in book form, or otherwise—to see what advice others had given on the subject of writing.
My primary motivation for not consulting any resources was simple: to share my take on how to write, not anyone else's.
In other words, the advice you'll find here consists of themes that have soaked into the cranium of yours truly over the years. Needless to say, those themes all originated *somewhere*. I definitely did not *discover* them; like everyone else, I soaked them up over the years from a variety of resources.
In yet other words, I will try to fish out—that is, out of the writer's swamp that is my cranium—the major strategies I use when going about the craft of writing.

The "How" (With A Bow)

As you read the advice that follows, you're bound to notice that a lot of the "how" of writing has to do with cultivating the writer's mindset. Sure, there are those rarest-of-rare individuals out there who are just born with the writer's mindset; I don't deny that, and in fact will have more to say on that exactly that in a bit.

But the fact is that most of the rest of us have to cultivate the writer's mindset—that's where the "how" of writing comes in. My hope in sharing this advice is that it'll help you along your journey as a writer; I was helped by many along the way. Now it's my turn to return the favor.

We Have Some Ground To Cover

We have a rather vast expanse lying ahead of us as we begin exploring writing strategies to level up your writing game. Let's start with taking in a bird's eye view of those strategies:

1. Listen To Yourself
2. Don't Listen To Yourself
3. Intend For Others
4. Extend Yourself
5. Write For Yourself
6. Write For The World
7. Get To Know Yourself
8. Read A Lot To Write Well
9. Diversify
10. Commit Professor Trimble's Book To Memory
11. Read Anything By Philip Bromberg
12. Fall In Love With The Allure Of Words
13. Seek Physicality In What You Write
14. Invest In A Bookshelf Or Two Or Three
15. Invest In A Good Dictionary

16. Invest In A Few Great Books On Writing
17. Read With A Highlighter In Hand
18. Revise What You Write
19. Become Your Own Editor
20. Collect Idioms
21. First Learn All The Rules Of Writing You Can
22. Then Write Unencumbered By Rules
23. Get To Know Your Left Brain
24. Get To Know Your Right Brain
25. Do Not Rush Your Writing
26. Learn About The Act Of Creation
27. Recognize The Limitations Of Digital Media
28. Believe In Yourself
29. Believe In The Goodness Of Mankind
30. Listen To Mark Knopfler Songs
31. Never Give Up On Your Search

A somewhat hefty list there, eh—I wasn't joking when I said that we have a *lot* ground to cover. So let's venture out and take on the writing strategies, one by one:

Be kind, for everyone you meet is fighting a harder battle.
- Plato

1. Listen To Yourself

First and foremost, start cultivating the belief that you have something to offer to the world. You have the perfect right to ask, "*Why should I believe you?*" I'm glad you asked, because the answer is simplicity itself: I *know* that you have something to offer to the world. The simple fact that you're a human is plenty right there to convince me that you've been endowed with what it takes to offer something to the world.

Cultivation Takes Some Getting Used To...

Remember, you will want to *truly* believe the same, at least to the same degree that I believe in *you*: Yes, it's never too early—or too late—to start cultivating a rock-solid belief in the trueness of what you're writing; after all, your writing *is* what you'll be offering to the world.

No doubt there's some work to be done to get there; all of us have to pay our dues. So what is it that you need to do to get there? It is simply this: Through your proverbial "*blood, sweat, and tears*", elevate your writing to its zenith; climb your own Pantheon.

Writing is not about making money; if it were, that's news at least to your blogger. Writing is about passion; it's all about busting your guts in the telling of the stories that you *have* to tell.

But what if we want to write about *basket*-weaving? Um, uh, so let's see.

How I Can Help?

So I may not be much help in that area, fine and noble though such endeavors surely must be. But let's look at it this way: Why don't we find a topic that you're passionate about, and then we take it from there? Yes, *yes*?

Great. I'm glad you asked. The rest of this essay is about *exactly* that, plus a bunch of related themes to help you grow as a writer.

The test of a first-rate intelligence is the ability to hold two opposed ideas in the mind at the same time, and still re-tain the ability to function.
~ F. Scott Fitzgerald (The Crack-Up)

2. Don't Listen To Yourself

I hear you say, "Okay, so this blogger guy Akram is plain nuts. I mean, for crying out loud: *First* he tells us to listen to ourselves, as in the previous advice. *Then* he turns right around and tells us to not listen to ourselves."

I also hear, "Come on, are you like that two-faced Janus or something? You know, one of those weirdo characters that we had to get ourselves acquainted with and suffer through—along with all those other, equally bizarre characters that plagued us —back when we took our ill-starred mythology class? I mean, *Make* up your mind, for crying out loud, 'cuz I got *way* better things to do with my time than watch this Janus-like soap opera!"

Whoah, wait up, gentle Reader. *Wait* up! I mean, hold your horses, of which there are *exactly* zero where I happen to live.

I beg of you to imagine how Charles Dickens—now *he* sure was a dickens of a writer—would have fared had he been pelted with a question like the following one from a potential publisher on first submitting his historical novel A Tale of Two Cities:

> *Publisher Chap: "Mr. Dickens, you really should make up your mind. Now was it the best of times or was it the worst of times? Surely it couldn't have been both."*
> *Charles Dickens: "My good fellow—Yo, what did you just say?"*

See, I told you so; there *is* a method to my madness. What I did above—I might as well spill the beans now—was to appeal to your finer sensibilities by hauling writing greatness into the fray: Mr. Dickens himself, yes, the dickens of a writer that he was. Look, if *Dickens* can speak of two seemingly opposite ideas in the same breath—kind of like how the Copenhagen interpretation of quantum mechanics implies that Schrödinger's cat can be simultaneously alive and dead—then surely a lesser writer like your blogger can do the same. Can I, please? *Pretty* please— with sugar on top—just this one time?

Now if only Dickens could've stopped short of bringing weirdos like Miss Havisham into the mix of his novel. Oh well, let's put this in perspective: *other* artists have committed far worst atrocities when *they* got carried away. I mean, wasn't there the famous artist—that Van Gogh dude, methinks—who cut off his own ear?

Oh. My. God.

One piece of advice: Don't do anything even *remotely* like that, *please* don't!

Again, may I suggest that you all, you aspiring writers, maintain lifestyles that are, um, slightly staider—in the *beginning* at least —and stay away from bizarre stuff like that. Once you're rich and famous, of course, all bets are off.

So you see, my essays—loony though they may appear on first blush—aren't *that* loony after all, especially when compared with what you read above; what I proposed, come to think of it, is what I would like to think of as falling within the rubric of "dialectic wisdom", and that, too in the realm of "dialectic wisdom"—well, I grant you that it's not *that* much of a dazzling display of dialectic brilliance, but *still...*

Come on, you've got to give your writer a break sometime.

The only way to avoid being miserable is not to have enough leisure to wonder whether you are happy or not.
~ George Bernard Shaw

3. Intend For Others

But how, you may well be wondering, could one ever intend for *others* when—with our ever-attendant and all-too-human foibles—we more often than not have trouble intending things for *ourselves*, let alone intending for *others*.

I mean, aren't we turning solipsism on its head here? Would we not be thereby turning the micro-cosmic into the macro-cosmic? Are we perhaps blazing anew the path shown to us by the legendary physicist Richard Feynman when he enlightened the world on the eerie phenomenon of electrons tunneling backward in time? Allow me to clarify—what I mean by *"Intend For Others"* is simply this: When you write, always treat others —after all, you're presumably writing not only for yourself, but *also* for others—as though they were *already* the selves that you wish for them to be, as if they had *already* attained that selfhood.

A little clarification, I hope, will help clear up the matter in tying this advice back to how it can inform your day-to-day writing journeys:

Always *write*—just as you *behave*—as if you readers *already* are the way you would wish for them to be: their best selves. Do that, and the rest will follow naturally.

Ah, but a man's reach should exceed his grasp,
Or what's a heaven for?
~ Robert Browning (in Andrea del Sarto)

4. Extend Yourself

How Writing Really Works

Work hard. Really, *really* hard. When you think you've written enough for the evening, write some more. Write until you are transported into the throes of fatigue and on the verge of collapsing into sleep right there at your keyboard, or next to your writing pad if you prefer the time-honored—and eminently sensible—way of writing in longhand; I'll have something to say about exactly that in a bit.

Where others may be tired and ready to call it a day, you're just

warming up—so if ever you entertained a thought otherwise, I invite you to think again. Yes, if you think that your day's worth of writing is done when you're merely tired, please think again. *That* isn't how writing works.
This is how writing works.

> *A writer is someone for whom writing is more difficult*
> *than it is for other people.*
> *- Thomas Mann*

As I revised this section—more on the crucial topic of *"revision"* later—something cool happened, as in: Oh. My. God.
So as I went online and looked up the quotation above—I had merely recalled it from memory and needed to make sure I was quoting it with integrity—my search randomly turned up an article by Joan Erakit: Being a Writer Is Hard. Joan's article is clearly written from the heart, and I've bookmarked it for later re-reading!
Here's the thing: Much as I told you earlier in this essay, I didn't consult any resources—online, or in book form, or otherwise—to see what advice *others* had given on the subject of writing and stuff like that. But what *do* you do when marvelous advice lands on your lap?

Sing Your Life Away With Words

What I say here can be taken literally as much as can be taken metaphorically. How you choose to view it is fully in your purview; the choice is yours to make.

Extend Yourself

Meanwhile, the advice we're talking about here (i.e. *"Extend Yourself"*) is so crucial that I'll now devote a good chunk of this essay to it: In other words, even if you don't take away anything else from this essay—and while I'd like to think that there at least a handful of points that you could take away—if you garner a single piece of advice, please make it this one:

Always remember that you were born to create great art. You, and you alone—you'll know this in your heart of hearts—are destined to create the art of prose that nobody else ever can.

Let me try to explain what I mean: So I rely on my readers to keep me educated. I try to avoid wallowing in my ignorance as often and as much as I can. In fact, this is as good a time to encourage you to feel free and contact me—I'm very approachable—thorough your comments, through Twitter, LinkedIn, etc.

Creating Great Art

Having got that out of the way, let's see if we can get a grip on what it means to create great art; and I'm not talking about Rembrandt or Van Gogh. Writing is—to my mind at least—as much an art as any other you care to name. So that, I would like to think, leads us to wonder what great writing looks like: Is there a litmus test—I offer profuse apologies for bringing up this topic to anyone who has reviled the study of Chemistry and deemed it a sordid mess—in which to dip a piece of writing and get the result out, yay or nay, something like the *Harry Potter* hat? I'm afraid not; at least there wasn't one the last time I checked.

And I'm not holding my breath for it either...

Taking A Leap Of Faith

My two cents' worth on this is that you'll know that you're on to writing good prose when what you write moves you. Once that happens, you know you've got something good going. At that point, do everything in your power to propel it forward till you reach the stars. Yes, this sounds nebulous, especially since you have an engineer and computer scientist—all rolled into one—serving this advice...

My point is that you have to take that leap of faith when you arrive at your springboard. When that happens, the need for the fabled litmus test—I offer profuse apologies for bringing up this topic a second time to anyone who has reviled the study of Chemistry and deemed it a sordid mess—that'll be your calculus for deciding whether what you've got in your hands is great or just so-so.

A Pyramid Of Writers

During literally the past 48 hours, I've had the pleasure of discovering a remarkable book by Stephen King: *On Writing: A Memoir Of The Craft.* Folks who know me may have been surprised—and possibly startled—to hear me mention the name of the maven of the horror genre. I never was into that genre, and am still not drawn to horror books in the least. But I have every reason to believe—and I say this based on the great things I've heard about King's books—that he is a great writer.

And while I've merely skimmed through a few sections of King's *On Writing,* I can already vouch for its stellar quality.

People don't just arrive at this out of nowhere. It takes years of cultivation.

Noblesse Oblige

Or maybe there *are* a few writers, a rare breed to be sure, who can bypass the whole process—somehow short-circuiting the seemingly unavoidable and admittedly arduous processes that writers of all stripes undergo in their training, maturation, refinement, and elevation of their prose into art form—being a rare breed that can rely on the artfully-linguistic, or perhaps linguistically-artful, primordial soup that brews unbidden in their brains.

If you're one of those, thank your lucky stars and know that you have to share your art with the world; and there are no ifs, ands, or buts here; and no, I'm not beguiling you by leading you down the alley of *noblesse oblige*—a French phrase that literally means "nobility obligates"—I assuredly am not. For one thing, I wasn't born into nobility or anything even *remotely* like that.

Noblesse What?

But yes, I've written those exact words—the phrase *noblesse oblige*—on a green board with a white chalk that I had ferreted out of a drawer in a table near which I happened to be seated, all alone in a classroom, in-between classes one afternoon as an undergraduate in Houston. I still haven't quite fathomed why I did that. All I recall is that I had to pick up the chalk and write that phrase; was this my way of getting it out of my system?

I was at that time—and remain to this day—an unabashed geek who revels in the joy of learning *and* helping others learn. So with my mental accelerator wired to the floor, as always, what I reflexively did that afternoon was perhaps the ideational equivalent of a tic, a reflexive and unbidden act of creativity, an ode that had to see the light of day.

But whatever it was, I still haven't unraveled the ball of yarn that beckoned me that afternoon. All I recall—and it's one of my clearest memories ever, just as if it took place yesterday, not on an afternoon a couple of decades ago—I distinctly recall doing so, unbidden.

We Joke Around Here And Such

Dear reader, you know me well, always joking and stuff, you know. Yeah, relax. After all, this is the playground of ideas which we—as the years have rolled by—have come to know as *ProgrammingDigressions*. You can always come here and bask in the sunshine of comfort, camaraderie, collegiality, kinship, and, most of all, for the unencumbered exchange of ideas. We're pretty much all geeks and nerds hanging out here in these quarters.

Okay, so as the resident impresario, I'll never allow this place to become seedy; if you wish to plant the seeds of fertile ideas, though, I'll take you by the hand and encourage you like you've never known encouragement before.

You trust me, and I trust you—you all are simply the best. I couldn't have asked for a better set of readers.

And to that end, to serve you as best as I humanly can—I consider that my top priority as I write every single sentence, every single word—I try my best to be forthright and express myself candidly. If ever I find even the slightest trace of deceit or deception make the faintest of inroads into what I write, I know that my writing life is done; as much as honesty is a salve, deception is poison.

A Solemn Note

I've got something solemn to share—So yes, I'm always joking in my essays and stuff like that; we're all a relaxed bunch here. But a time arrives one is compelled to make a statement, and when your heart is in the throes of breaching self-disclosure; this is such a time, and I feel compelled to engage in some self-disclosure.

I. Am. Dead. Serious.

As you read what I'm about to say, please keep these *two* points in mind and you'll be good: Self-disclosure. Allegory. To that I'll add a third: *Parable.*

Okay, for the sake of accuracy, let's quickly revise what we just read: Please keep the *three* points

above—*Self-disclosure*; *Allegory*; and *Parable*—in mind and you'll be good.

Beholding A Spectacle

But first, you need to know something... No matter *what* happens, no matter where we all end up—closer still to one another or perhaps farther away—please keep what I'm about to say close to your heart. I will, as ever, remain forthright and candid in all matters except one this one, and to which I happen to be privy: I've intimately known someone who can tap into the artfully-linguistic—or linguistically-artful if you will—primordial soup that brews in unbroken cycles, unbeknownst and unbidden even to them. I was in awe as my eyes beheld the creation of art of the highest order.

Words Failed Me...

I suspect that I'm not doing a good job at all of describing the experience of witnessing someone in the midst of the act of effortlessly producing art, hammering out prose just as fast as they could type, and doing all that with effortless ease. I was in awe. I felt like when I was a little boy, gazing heavenward at the billions and billions of shining stars, lighting up our elegant universe.

I said above, and you probably noted as much when I said it —that they were *"doing all that with effortless ease"*—and it still rings true with me. Could it be that they were like the proverbial duck, appearing calm but furiously paddling away with their webbed feet...

I doubt it, though the duck metaphor did cross my mind so, for what it's worth, I wished to run it by you. We're talking full disclosure here, anyway, right?

Describing An Artist At Work

But whatever words I could conceivably choose with which to paint a half-decent picture of a true artist at work, I already know that the effort is futile; I will invariably fail at describing it adequately enough. What I'm trying to describe borders on the outer boundaries of reason, entering the realm of ESP (aka Extrasensory Perception.)

But I have seen it with more than my eyes; I've *felt* it with my sense. So while I can't say that I've seen it in corporeal action, I can say with utmost confidence that I've witnessed it in action; like when you wake up from a dream and know what you've witnessed and yet you're unable to fully retrace the steps through which it all happened.

The mere realization of something so subtle and yet blindingly obvious taking place before my eyes nearly made me faint. I may even have gone into a syncope. It's a blur, but when I came to, I realized that I had witnessed true art being created before my eyes. I was in awe, and I wanted to tell them—I wanted to shout at the top of my lungs—that they truly had the rarest-of-rare quality in having what it takes to write words that drip with gold, verses that shimmer with the sheen of silver.

But I couldn't. Somehow it all eluded me. I'm sorry, I really am.

A Promise

But you have my word: When I meet them again another time —and I sure hope I do so because it was a deeply moving honor unlike any I've known in my life—I just might have better luck. Then again, I might not. But I'll give it my best shot; I'll try my best to let them know that our world needs to know about their art. They can make spirits sing and they can make hearts weep. They have what it takes. And yes, they have the moral responsibility to share their art—their prose—with the world and lift it above the humdrum of the noise of everyday life. When that happens, we'll no longer need to live lives of quiet desperation. I look forward to the dawn of such a day, a day that'll be its usual selfsame self and yet find itself tinged with dripping gold and bathed in shimmering silver.

Okay, you all can breathe easy now and, in turn, so can I. Whew, was that intense or what? I don't know about you, but I was mostly holding my breath all the while I wrote the couple of paragraphs above as I got ready to ship them to you.

Divulging Some Matters

And truth be told, I even debated a few times in the first place whether I should even *divulge* what I just did. But of course I've gone ahead and done exactly that. And you know what, at the end of the day, we're all in this together; if we don't share our experiences freely with one another in sincere acts of helping one another grow, then much will have been lost, or even worse, never even gained, though what was never gained can perhaps be regained.

Yes, there are those rare souls who truly have what it takes of tap into phenomenal powers of creativity and commune with their fertile imaginations where most of the rest of us would simply fall flat on our faces, tripping all over ourselves in our zeal.

We, Mere Mortals

And then there are the rest of us. We, mere mortals. I know this all to well because I've fallen and bruised my face from lack of dexterity in weaving words into strands of gold that might have captivated my own heart; that is a first, essential step; but if I can't quite take that step yet, then I know that I have a long way to go still. But that's okay. I take heart in the wise Chinese saying that the journey of a thousand miles begins with a single step. And indeed, it does.

So not to worry even *one* bit; we're in this together. We'll help one another create absolutely the best art that we're capable of creating, just you and I—be it be the loveliest prose you could set your eyes on or be it code of breathtaking beautiful that make your heart skip on beholding it. You have my word. If anyone asks who told you so, would you please tell them that

Akram did, and on good authority, too? Thank you.

Sprezzatura

Let me close this thought with an example with which I was recently enlightened by a reader—a reader of these essays who just happens to also be a most highly esteemed friend—about the nature of great art. They enlightened me on how
The Italians have a word for it: *sprezzatura*. Making something difficult look easy is the mark of a truly gifted performer or writer.
Then I got to thinking that I have a good friend (based in Canada for many years now) who is originally from Italy. Who better to get insight into an Italian word than someone who grew up speaking Italian. So *that's* where I went next. On reaching out to my Italian friend, I got a gracious and detailed response.
For reasons of confidentiality, I can't share the entire response (personal communication). But here is a part—intact—of what my friend wrote back to me:

> *...The word [sprezzatura] is actually not a common one in Italian. It's essentially the ability to hide one skill by performing an act so effortlessly that it looks easy. Think a great painter making it look so easy but when you try to do the same it looks like a 5-year-old painted it. I would consider it one of the highest compliments.*

Ah, if only *I* could set my sights so high.

Poetry creates the myth, the prose writer draws its portrait.
- Jean-Paul Sartre

5. Write For Yourself

You all know me well as the software craftsman that I am, to which credentials I'd like to add—with obvious pride—that I'm also a nerd, and a technologist whose imagination has recently been given a pair of wings through the aegis of a book that goes by the name of *Plato and the Nerd* (The MIT Press), and I'm a programming languages enthusiast, too.

But gosh, surely, *I'm* not a writer—remember everything we read earlier about how I sometimes suspect that you all would rather have my essays towed away, and at my expense, too? Or something like that, right? Or can somebody actually convince me that I am a, gulp, bona fide' writer?
But hey, I take heart in what Ralph Waldo Emerson's observation when he had memorably advised to

     Hitch your wagon to a star

That, surely is a dream floating far away from me, ever so elusively; like the butterfly which hasn't alighted, yet, on the flower on which it was destined to alight. Ah, if only I could be that kind of a writer. But wait, maybe I am one, already and just don't know it?
You see, I tried my hand at rhyming verse in an earlier essay— and folks haven't pelted me with tomatoes, so far, anyway—so maybe I could take that as a sign that I'm a poet and I just didn't know it? Hmm...

Yeah, this is *precisely* what happens anytime I entertain discursive forays into solipsism and stuff like that; *cool* though it surely is, it also makes me think back to my undergraduate days taking a class in Philosophy...

As a side note, I came first in my class—goodness, come to think of it, the enrollment in the Philosophy class that semester was quite massive; I had at *least* 150 classmates. I don't quite recall whether that class was oversubscribed just that semester or something, but I distinctly recall the auditorium in which I used to sit—my classmates and I, packed like sardines in a cavernous auditorium—taking in each word of my professor with rapt attention. Indeed, your blogger is just plain nuts.
Hey, methinks I doth digress. Nevermore. Quoth the Raven.

(Okay, okay—hey, *you* wise guy snickering there in the back row —I *do* know my raven from my airplane, *okay*? It's just that I can't find the emoticon for a bird, let alone a raven, in the palette available to me. Your artist has come up short; can you, like, *live* with that, for crying out loud?)

Letters are among the most significant memorial a person can leave behind them.
-Johann Wolfgang von Goethe

6. Write For The World

Question your assumptions and open your heart; when you do, your writing will open up for you. And when that happens— when your writing opens up and unto you—you will know that it's time to open your writing to the world in which we live.
Allow plans larger than you own to fold, as they say.
And be patient. Miracles will take place before your very eyes.

Be yourself; everyone else is already taken.
- Oscar Wilde

7. Get To Know Yourself

No matter what comes your way. No matter what life hands to you, always remember this: You, and you alone, are destined to create what nobody else will ever be able to create. All this follows from keep the following adage close to heart:

To Your Own Self Be True

I was tempted to call this section *"Believe In Yourself"* but that sounded too Tony Robbins. So there.

The Growth Mindset

Of course, there will be times—for writers and everyone else—

when you'll be compelled to seek growth; it's an all-too-natural process. Just as a snake sheds its skin, we humans, too, outgrow our old selves and need to shed them; we, too, need to grow into new states of being. So should you wish to *change*, not to worry a bit. I found some advice on exactly that, too:

> *To change one's life:*
> *1. Start immediately.*
> *2. Do it flamboyantly.*
> *3. No exceptions.*
> *- William James*

Wow, did you notice that James had his stuff down as a list, did you now? Pretty impressive, I would say. I mean, we nerds actually could've made an engineer out of James, what with our propensity for list-making at the drop of a hat?

Resident Engineer (Or Writer?)

Just imagine: William James the resident *engineer.* Hmm... While good for us all who dwell in the realm of technology, and should such a happenstance ever have transpired—i.e. William James having a change of heart and devoting his life to the pursuit of engineering—all that may not have gone over too well with the Psychology department at Harvard University. I mean, who would've gone on to write *The Principles of Psychology* with which to make legions of future students (in the ivy-lined classrooms or otherwise) fall asleep?

8. Read A Lot To Write Well

> *It took me four years to paint like Raphael, but a lifetime to paint like a child.*
> *~ Pablo Picasso*

Perhaps I'm stating the obvious. But there's simply no substitute for reading widely, even as you read deeply—it will do wonders for your own writing, guaranteed, or your money back. Um, or something *like* that.

Hopefully, this piece of advice is descriptive enough, so I won't elaborate beyond that.

Painting is poetry that is seen rather than felt, and poetry is painting that is felt rather than seen.
- Leonardo da Vinci

9. Diversify

Read widely; do not limit yourself.
Broaden your horizons; the sky truly *is* the limit.
Reach for the stars.
(I owe the genesis of this piece of advice to my friend, the late John Vlissides of IBM's T.J. Watson Research Center—the "V" in "GHJV" (Gamma, Helm, Johnson, and Vlissides), the inimitable Gang of Four (GoF)—who enlightened the world with gifts that I have seen in rare, few others. Vlissides remains one of all-time programming heroes of all time, right up there with Guy Steele, who, by the way, is widely regarded as the father of Common Lisp, and just happens to be the lead author of the Java Language

Specification).

Art is not what you see, but what you make others see.
- Edgar Degas

10. Commit Professor Trimble's Book To Memory

Should you take away from this essay only one book to get for yourself, *please* make it *Writing with Style: Conversations on the Art of Writing* by John R. Trimble. I refer to the volume fondly as *WWS*. My writing life can be cleanly divided—much as the World Wars (WW) divided history into pre- and post-WW—into pre- and post-*WWS*. What more can I say? I adore that book.

11. Read Anything By Philip Bromberg

Never apologize for showing feeling. When you do so, you apologize for the truth.
~ Benjamin Disraeli

Sublime Prose On Display

Should you wish to see examples of truly sublime prose on display—and while YMMV, I encourage you to try the strategy of learning-from-examples—look no further than the work of Philip M. Bromberg. His writing is replete with honesty, humor, and thoughtfulness. I've written about Bromberg's work in several of my earlier essays; for example, you can check out this essay which explores the nexus between beautiful computer code and beautiful prose.

And since we are—and will be—seeing Dickinson's genius on display (in this essay) by way of her verses of poetry, it's only fair that you have the chance, too, to briefly check out the work of Bromberg, a more-contemporary genius; though he may not not *quite* be in the league of Dickinson, surely he isn't *too* far behind either. Interestingly enough, Bromberg has written quite a bit of and about Dickinson, for example. On top of that, as if this wasn't a barrel of monkeys already, for crying out loud, *yet* another individual, a professor at UPenn (Max Cavitch), decided to join the fray—in "meta" or "recursive" fashion—and written about *his* (i.e. Bromberg's) writing about her (i.e. Dickinson's) work. Fancy that.

An Example

In my book, Bromberg is the master of crafting seamless prose, which is something that I've tried to explain in an essay elsewhere, and which was in the context of chatting about his book entitled *Awakening the Dreamer*.

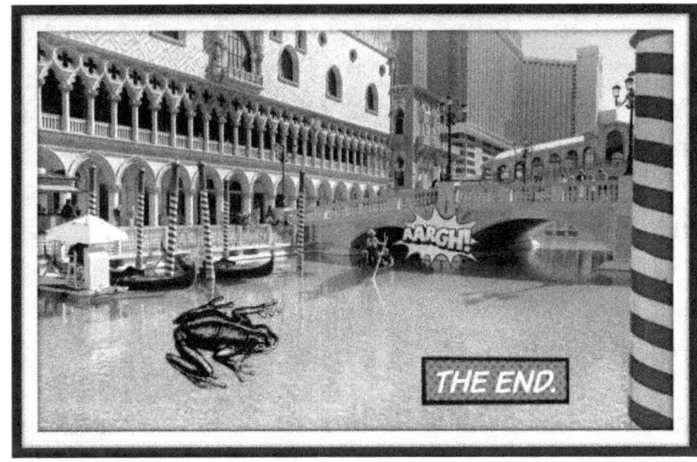

Voldemort, In Reverse

Hmm... "*Voldemort In Reverse*"? What in the world could be going on here?

So we had got to talking some about that holothurian critter above, whose name, by the way, sounds right up there—actually right *down* there since we're speaking of ocean-dwelling critters —with another equally-hideous-sounding name: coelacanth. What are those marine biologist guys and gals thinking when they cook up such outlandish names?

Just *look* at what those marine biologists have already thrown at us simple folks—holothurian, coelacanth, elasipodida, pelago-thuriidae—I mean, sheesh... Where does this all stop, if *ever* it does? Next, we'll be hearing about critters with names such as *Arabor, Dor-lómin, Mithrin, Elrond*, and stuff like that. Now's the time to turn a leaf. Or, "*Good grief, Charlie Brown.*" (We won't let you down.)

Marine Biologists: Please Meet Bilbo Baggins

I mean, why can't they use honest-to-goodness names that we folks—all of the *rest* of us who live on Main Street—can relate to as well? How about Bilbo, or Baggins? Better yet, let's have our esteemed marine biologists name the next creature they discover... Yes! *That's* it: Bilbo Baggins. Maybe even Gollum. I mean, is that memorable or what?

Now try remembering a name like holothurian, coelacanth, elasipodida, pelagothuriidae. *Exactly*, that's all I'm saying—just sayin', if anybody would only listen. Sigh.

He Who Must Not Be Named

Anyhow, speaking of the holothurian, doesn't it's philosophy of life remind you of "he who must not be named"? You know who I'm talking about here, don't you? In case you've been living under a rock and somehow managed to evade exposure to the phenomena that is the *Harry Potter* series, *here's* what's up...

Okay, so I will toss caution to the wind and somewhat grudgingly divulge the name—notwithstanding the dire warnings of doing *exactly* that—of "he who must not be named": Voldemort, pestiferous dimwit if ever there was one. I mean, think about it this way:

Voldemort—sneaky and proactive baddy that he was—was kind of like a holothurian in *reverse*, having planned ahead by splitting and stashing. Grisly stuff there for sure.

But hey, any given holothurian out there (that gelatinous sea creature) is sort of a *reactive* Voldemort, splitting itself into smithereens when it finds itself in mortal danger.

How Does He Do It?

I have but a single word of reaction—one word, nothing less, nothing more—to describe what Bromberg manages to do with his "word-painting" or "word-sculpting", if that's what you wish to call it: *Wow!*

I don't know how he does it, but he does; his awesome writing makes me turn green with envy.

Frankly, Bromberg immediately comes to mind as the other notable writer—in addition to the brilliant mathematician-philosopher Bertrand Russell—who appears to be as fond of using those sparkly em-dashes in their writing as your blogger is.

Read up Bromberg's writings; I suspect that the writer in you will thank you for the wonders it will do for *your* writing.

Education is an admirable thing, but it is well to remember from time to time that nothing that is worth knowing can be taught.
~ Oscar Wilde, (The Critic as Artist)

12. Fall In Love With The Allure Of Words

I'm just nuts about words. There are no two ways about it.

Please, I beg of you: Give yourself permission to fall in love with the allure of words. This allure is the surest cure for a flagging

spirit, the purest salve that'll give you endurance, sustaining you during times when even you begin to doubt yourself.
How does that grab you? If you find yourself resonating with the words above, I suggest that you grab it right back: Run to your nearest brick-and-mortar bookstore and grab a copy of a great thesaurus: My favorite is *The Synonym Finder* Revised Edition (by J. I. Rodale), although the highly regarded *Roget's International Thesaurus*, 7th Edition Revised (by Barbara Ann Kipfer) —I used to have a copy of it back when I lived in Minnesota—is pretty good, too.

Go grab a copy of either one of two thesauri above and knock yourself out.

13. Seek Physicality In What You Write

No tears in the writer, no tears in the reader. No surprise in the writer, no surprise in the reader.
- Robert Frost

You simply *have* to imbue your prose with emotion; if your prose isn't suffused with the physicality of feelings and tinged by your true feelings, it ain't going anywhere. Period.
Try to imagine what it would be like to read cold and forbidding whale-like paragraphs. Does it sound inviting? Indeed, it does not. Now put yourself in your *reader's* shoes, and you'll get an idea of what you need to do to fix the problem: Bring your to life with vivid prose that lives and breathes the life you'll be putting into it.
Yep, it behooves us *all* to dig deeper into this area of writing which is, oddly enough, sometimes overlooked.

14. Invest In A Bookshelf

Or Two Or Three

The oldest books are only just out to those who have not read them.
- Samuel Butler

Obvious or trite though this advice may sound, please follow up on it: Invest in a bookshelf, or two, or three. Your (writing) life depends on it. This is vital stuff. You can cruise the web all day long, reading online, but there never *was*—and likely never *will* be—a substitute for physical books. Take this from a writer who also happens to be an engineer and computer scientist.
Please get yourself a bookshelf, or two, or three. It really doesn't matter what kind of bookshelves you invest in: get them from *IKEA*, your local *Target* or *Walmart*. What *does* matter is that you line your home with a bookshelf, or two, or three.
Okay, so I'll stop sounding like a broken record now.
Now that we're in business—at least I hope we are, with you having heeded my words above—shall we take up the fine matter of *lining* them up with some books?

15. Invest In A Good Dictionary

I often quote myself; it adds spice to my conversation.
~ George Bernard Shaw

Ah yes, to fall in love with words through contact with the pages of a dictionary that you can hold in your hands. While it may sound old-fashioned, there's simply *no* substitute for physical contact with a tangible—compared to an online—dictionary. The experience of interacting with the physicality of a good dictionary simply can't be recreated by its online counterpart, especially when you're learning words for the first time; if all you're doing is looking up a dictionary to *verify* your understanding of a particular word, by all means fire up your web browser and look up the word in an online dictionary; I do that *all* the time.

So won't you please—pretty please, with sugar on top—invest in a dictionary, a *really* good one? Thank you, your cooperation is appreciated.

And don't forget to write to me with your experience when your investment (in a corporeal dictionary) is repaid in spades.

When I have a little money, I buy books; if I have any left, I buy food and clothes.
~ Erasmus

16. Invest In A Few Great Books On Writing

Okay, let's go grab more stuff with which to line our empty bookshelves, cool? Heading over to the bookstore now.

So this advice—while it may appear to be along the lines of my advice in the previous item—is actually *far* more fun. Yep, we'll have you run to your nearest—or *farthest*, if you so wish—brick-and-mortar bookstore and have yourself some browsing fun. I mean I'll be the last one to stand between you and your getting good exercise as you take a brisk walk (or leisurely stroll, as your mood suits you) to the bookstore at the farthest corner of the earth.

One way or another, once you're in the bookstore, you'll inevitably find books on writing style that speak to you, because, as they say, different strokes for different folks. When you find those books, invest in them. You'll be more than repaid in the dividends you reap down the road.

17. Read With A Highlighter In Hand

Reinforcing Hawking and Gödel, Wolpert uses a similar self-embedding to conclude that predicting the future is I not only use all the brains I have, but all that I can borrow.
- Woodrow Wilson

Indeed, please make it a point to read with a highlighter in hand. It'll do wonders for your writing life in truly helping you grok the content in a way that just might surprise you; yes, highlighting isn't for students only. So please read with a highlighter in hand.

You *know* what I'm saying, right? Yes, *yes*, you nod your head in affirmation. Yep, you got it: Don't just *hold* the highlighter in your hand. Actually, remove the cap—or click the clicker if your highlighter is one of those retractable kind—and *start* highlighting. Once you start, you ain't gonna want to stop. Yay, have .

Make the book you're reading your own marked-up, lit-up piece of art. The book should cease to be a faceless stranger. Make the book your *friend*. Have a dialog with it. It's quite all right; nothing schizophrenic about it. Relax.

Half my life is an act of revision.
~ John Irving

18. Revise What You Write

A dear friend—one of the best writers on this planet—once wrote to me, saying

> *They say that revision is the heart and soul of writing.*
> *(Personal communication with author, I mean, blogger;*
> *the two are the same, though, right?)*

I still find myself nodding in complete agreement; I can't of anything to add to the elegant simplicity of the advice above!

If anything, I'll merely add an *afterthought*, which taps into my engineering and programming background: As any fellow programmer—with the notable exception of legendary computer scientist Donald Knuth—will care to admit, our first pass at writing any computer program can result in sloppy code. But obviously we don't stop there; in fact, our first pass is merely the *beginnings* of creating a computer program, and which serves as the launchpad for refinement-unto-refinement-unto... Ad nauseum, until we have a finished product; a robust computer program.

19. Become Your Own Editor

The limits of my language are the limits of my mind. All I know is what I have words for.
- Ludwig Wittgenstein

But Akram, I don't have the *budget* to invest in a course or two for becoming an editor—or for that matter, the time to take a class. Relax. What I've got here is *far* easier than what you might be thinking. All I've got in mind here is simply this: *Each* word of *every* sentence that you write needs to pull its weight; deadweight simply doesn't fly in the realm of great prose.
Keep that in mind, and you'll be golden.

20. Collect Idioms

Get into a rut early: Do the same process the same way. Accumulate idioms. Standardize. The only difference(!) between Shakespeare and you was the size of his idiom list —not the size of his vocabulary.
- Alan Perlis (Yale University computer science professor, first-ever recipient of the Turing Award)

Herein lies a motherlode of writing wisdom, beckoning for you to mine it for its hidden nuggets. As you go about embracing this crucial advice, be especially mindful—in the words of the inimitable poet-genius Emily Dickinson—of the message she had in saying that "Except for its marauding hand, It *had been*

heaven below" (italics mine).
Once you get that, it's off to the proverbial races.

*Be careful about reading health books. You may die of a
misprint.*
~ Mark Twain

21. Learn All The Rules Of Writing You Can

The whole point of this advice is to get the rules of writing style
—as many of them as you can get under your belt (for my male
readers) or your obi (for my female readers)—so ingrained into

your consciousness that you can use them reflexively. The writing advice above leads naturally to the piece of advice in the next item.

22. Then Write Unencumbered By Rules

Literature is strewn with the wreckage of men who have minded beyond reason the opinions of others.
- Virginia Woolf

If your mind is occupied all the time with considerations of whether you're violating the rules of writing—and they *are* valid concerns, please don't get me wrong—as you write every single sentence, then the writing process is going to be ploddingly painful. To comfort you, I offer that I, too, have felt that pain, albeit in a different context: that of writing code in the C++ programming language

Before any of you C++ programming aficionados get all roiled up by my preceding comment, let me assure you that I wish C++ programming the very best; let's just say that when I discovered the Java programming language, I never looked back. The story is rather long, and I refer anyone with an interest in this particular digression to an essay that I had written earlier; it's one of the handful of occasions where I've touched upon that topic.

In sum, internalize the rules of writing until they become second nature; aim to put yourself in a position where you don't even have to think about rules; they inform your writing unbidden. In other words, work hard to get those rules engrained deeply enough where they become like the air you breathe; exactly, in the same way you don't notice your breathing, you shouldn't have to notice that you're applying this rule or that at any point of your writing process.

I'm sticking by my story even if it reeks of heresy and would be *branded* as such by a purist grammarian.

23. Get To Know Your Left Brain

*A change in the weather is sufficient to recreate the world
and ourselves.
- Marcel Proust*

Getting to know your left brain is, of course, the realm of logical thinking. Don't ignore. Remember, though, that writing greatness does not lie here. It is a start. By the same token, this is an important area that deserves serious attention: this is the realm of writing tasks such as creating a coherent outline for you writing task at hand, making sure you supply plenty of arguments to bolster your claims, and other stuff (essential) stuff like that.

24. Get To Know Your Right Brain

*Imagination is more important than knowledge. Knowledge is limited. Imagination encircles the world.
~ Albert Einstein*

Just as there is art in magic, there is magic in art. As a writer, ignore this dictum at your own peril.
Find your muse: be it soul-moving sonatas or masterpieces of paintings. Then let those sonatas and masterpieces move your *writing*.

What makes the desert beautiful is that somewhere it hides a well.
- Antoine de Saint-Exupery

25. Do Not Rush Your Writing

The best I can do here is point you to some fabulous advice I came across several years ago:

Successful students don't spend much more time working than their peers, they just spend their working time smarter. Take three days to write your short papers—your mind, your body, and your professors will thank you.

Also, check Cal Newport's *Item # 41: Use Three Days to Write a Paper* from his book entitled *How to Win at College: Surprising Secrets for Success from the Country's Top Students* (Crown)

What works for student sure can work for writers, too.

26. Learn About The Act Of Creation

Art is never finished, only abandoned.

~ Leonardo da Vinci (1452 – 1519)

Writing *is* creating. Invest some time exploring the spirit of contradiction and, even more importantly, set aside time daily to meditating on why true art is never finished.

Reading, after a certain age, diverts the mind too much from its creative pursuits. Any man who reads too much and uses his own brain too little falls into lazy habits of thinking, just as the man who spends too much time in the theater is tempted to be content with living vicariously instead of living his own life.
~ Albert Einstein

27. Recognize The Limitations Of Digital Media

This particular advice might strike you as a tad Philistine, especially after having read my recent essays on a brand new book entitled *Plato and the Nerd* (by Edward Ashford Lee, published by The MIT Press)—a bit more on it shortly (specifically in the advice coming up under the 31st item: "Never Give Up On Your Search"). But quickly, here again were the essays devoted to unraveling the nuances of *Plato and the Nerd*, each of which essay you'll enjoy, dare I say:

Read up at your leisure the very first deep dive into its wherewithal and gestalt

Follow up that deep dive with a slightly different perspective on its offerings

Finally, settle down for a relaxed home stretch that's suffused with some slight poignancy

Going back to my comment above regarding how this particular piece of advice might strike you as a tad Philistine, here's what I had in mind: As a matter of fact, nothing could be farther from the truth—since we spoke of *Plato and the Nerd* just a breath away, suffice it to say that you'll benefit tremendously from a deliberate study of what Edward has to say on the concept of "continuums" in that book I just mentioned. Rather than elaborate on that concept—as well as a ton of others which are helping me hugely in my life as a writer—I refer you to a perusal of the three essays above. They will get you situated with a hopefully fuller appreciation of what all the remarkable volume has to offer to you, as a writer and thinker.

28. Believe In Yourself

> *To lose one's faith surpasses*
> *The loss of an estate,*
> *Because estates can be*
> *Replenished, — faith cannot.*
> *- Emily Dickinson*

Touchy-feely though this advice may sound, it is important.

Linger over it. And to that end, I invite you to spend some time soaking in the intent of the two quotes atop this piece of advice.

29. Believe In The Goodness
Of Mankind

Are friends delight or pain?
Could bounty but remain
- Emily Dickinson

The day I stop believing in the goodness of mankind will be the day I stop writing. Period. And I don't see that happening anytime soon; yes, despite all the doom and gloom that envelopes our society under darker clouds by the day.
I believe in the goodness of mankind—*and* womankind, to be sure. It's part of the fuel that serves to propel everything that I write, and to inform everything that I do.

30. Listen To Mark Knopfler Songs

The historian records, but the novelist creates.
~ E. M. Forster

Reader: "Oh. My. God."
Blogger: "Relax. I need some information first. Just the basic facts."
Reader: "Stop in the name of all things sacred."
Blogger: "But why?"
Reader: "Why? *I'll* tell you why: At the rate you're going... The next thing we know, you'll start pontificating on ritornellos!"
Blogger: "Rita-who?"
Reader: "Rito*rnellos*, dude. Aren't you educated or something?"
Blogger: "Oh, *those*. Yeah, yeah"
Reader: "Good grief, for crying out loud."

Reader, again: "This guy is just plain *nuts*."
Blogger: "Right, so I was saying..."
Reader: "There. He. Goes. *Again!*"

Appreciating The Lyricism Of Music

Listen up, because here's the deal: While *I* may know nothing about music, my *Mom* does, so you be careful about what you say, hey! And while I have a biological mother—the sweetest soul on earth—who enjoys music but doesn't know the rubrics of music (neither to I, for that matter), don't forget that I *also* have an adopted Mom, another truly gracious, caring, and refined soul. And dude, *she* knows music backward and forward. That's right, so you better think twice before making snide remarks as you did above.

And Appreciating The Music That Dwells Everywhere

My adopted Mom has taught me a thing or two about what it means to appreciate music. While sheet music may forever remain an enigma in my mind (Greek that it is to me), I have, however, learned from Mom—and continue to learn from her *every* single day that I'm alive on this planet—something about the music that lives in the recesses of prose. Yes, these are lessons on the music that dwells in prose, waiting in the wings, poised to take flight and soar to heights unlike anything we've seen before.
Much more than even all *that*, they are—those lessons from Mom—lessons in *life* itself.
Therefore, you be a good boy—and *you* be a good girl—and listen up to what I've got to say, hey now.

An Invitation

With that, I invite you to go out and learn something about

the genius of Mark Knopfler. He is a singer-songwriter, guitarist (of the British music group Dire Straits) who has already made several appearances in ProgrammingDigressions essays. Knopfler's songs are deeply symbolic, steeped—soaked, drenched-but-not-bedraggled, if you know what I mean—in the syrup of some of the most thoughtful lyrics you'll ever have heard. Ever. *Really* great stuff; well worth your while.

Check out his songs. If you find yourself resonating with their lyrics—*I* surely have—allow their lyricism to leave their impression on your writing. Your writing *just* might become that much lyrical; I sure hope *mine* will, one day, if perhaps in some small way only.

You May Also Wish To Listen To...

I'm not trying to sell the songs of Knopfler; *far* from it. Come on; we're democratic here, after all, unlike some other places.

And that leads me to make mention of how the title of this section—*"Listen To Mark Knopfler Songs"*—just as easily might have been any one of the following, depending on *your* taste in music:

- Listen To Chopin Nocturnes
- Hum to Sarah McLachlan Tunes
- Sway To Kishore Kumar Melodies
- Lend An Ear To Elton John Ballads

All I'm saying is this: allow music to hold at least some sway over what you write. You don't *have* to, but give it a try; you don't have anything to lose, except perhaps a fistful of dollars you'll spend buying some songs to listen to.

And hey, if you're cheap like I am, all you have to do is turn on the radio and listen to some sad songs, because they say so much. Oh *yes* they do.

In yet other words, see if you can swizzle some music into your prose; your writing just may take a turn for the lyrical. Even better, the admixture might work miracles for your writing; it just might.

As For Alvin And The Chipmunks

Whatever you do, I beg of you to please never, *ever* listen to Alvin and the Chipmunks—those annoying, anthropomorphic chipmunks: Alvin, Simon and Theodore—because if I find out that you do, I'm going to hang up my hat and you won't get another essay out of me (*or* out of my hat, notwithstanding my being a non-magician.)
Exactly, you ain't gonna see no more essays from yours truly.
I mean, *sheesh*... Don't their grating-mechanical songs—*if* they can even be elevated to being called songs—just drive you nuts? It's like being forced to hear someone drag a sharp set of nails across a chalkboard.
Yikes. *I'm* outta here; someone holler and I'll be back when their infernal music stops.
Can you even *imagine* what irrevocable havoc such stuff could wreak with your prose? All I'm saying is this: you have to draw the line *somewhere*
(In full disclosure, we were just having some fun here: I have nothing whatsoever against those adorable-and-*pesky*-at-the-same-time chipmunks.)

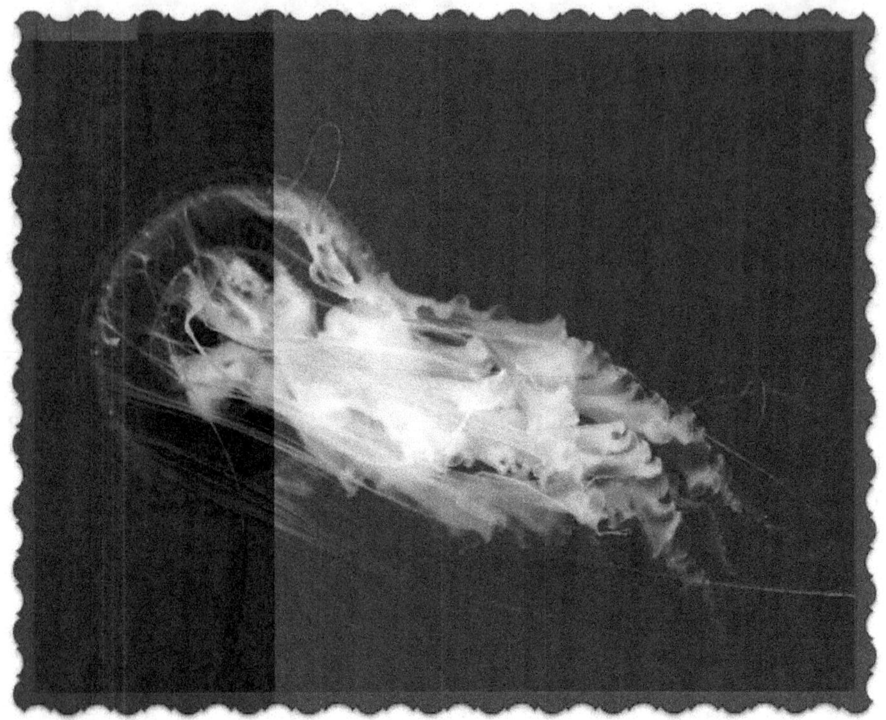

Consistency is the last refuge of the unimaginative.
- Oscar Wilde

31. Never Give Up On Your Search

This one stands for itself: Enough said, amirite?
Onward.

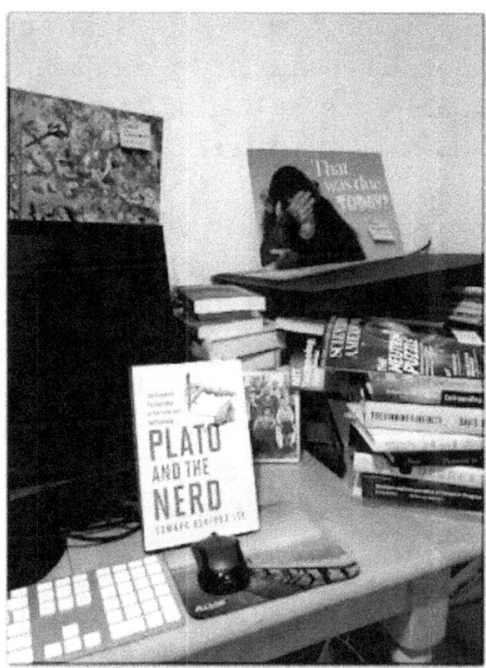

I Had Saved The Best For Last

I had saved the best for last: So the search I've got in mind here is the one for that oh-so-elusive spark. This is the spark that will unlock your muse; it will give your imagination the wings with which to soar heavenward; and yes, it will also validate your belief in yourself (as a writer, among other things). Imagine that, all rolled into one.

Allow me to illustrate this seemingly nebulous advice—though to my mind it is *anything* but—with a personal anecdote. I'm acutely aware of how I wear you all out by my rambling, but what I'm going to tell you now is, I believe, substantial enough to merit your attention: I never give up on my search for the spark. I hung in there through the good times, and the bad.

And Then It Happened...

Then, one Sunday afternoon, I walked into our local brick-and-mortar *Barnes & Noble* bookstore (*B&N*). I can't quite describe it all—I begin to choke up even as I try to recall details of that fateful trip to the B&N—because that moment was ineffable, suspended at it *still* is in my mind its selfsame animation. Frozen in time.

I don't know how it happened, it all took place so quick. But it remains etched in my mind, in my soul. So I was drawn—as surely as the moth which is drawn to its fateful embrace with fiery embers that will ultimately scorch it to death—to a bookshelf that held for me the gift of a lifetime.

With my right hand I reached out into the rack and held the gem in my hands. From that moment onwards—though I didn't the timer on my stopwatch—it took all of some 30 odd seconds of flipping through that book's pages and I knew it right then and there: I had found *my* spark.

The Prize Was In My Hands

Before rushing to the row of cashier's desk to check out the prize that I held clenched in my hands, I looked again at the book to make sure I wasn't dreaming. So I asked my wife to pinch me. She did. And I said, Ow! It was *then* that I knew I was fully awake. I'll add this much—in the spirit of full disclosure—that I *did* also cast a furtive glance at my hands just to make sure they weren't scorched. They were not. *Whew!*

Evidently, this moth was the one that got away. Drawn though it was to its fiery embrace with the spark, this time the moth was not so much as singed. Its integrity—wings, spirit, soul—remained intact even as it made contact with the fire which was going to light up its life.

I had found my spark, *woohoo!*

And Then It Began...

Yes, it was precisely *then* then it began...
Plato and the Nerd: The Creative Partnership of Humans and Technology (The MIT Press) by Edward Ashford Lee
And yes, as they say, the rest is history: I went on to write not one but a whopping *three* essays as a paen to my spark.
No doubt, many of you may already know all about those (three) essays; it wasn't *that* long ago that they appeared on this blog (which we fondly call Programming Digressions around here). But for our new readers—the thousands and thousands who I'm happy to see pile on to partake of the exchange of ideas that is the *raison d'être* of ProgrammingDigressions—I owe you a quick roundup.

Roundup By Way Of Three Pointers

Without further ado, what follow below are directions—one

each to the three essays—which will whisk you away to some reading fun that is waiting for you:

1. Read up at your leisure the very first deep dive into its where-withal and gestalt

2. Follow up that deep dive with a slightly different perspective on its offerings

3. Finally, settle down for a relaxed home stretch that's suffused with some slight poignancy

Have fun reading up the essays above. Remember, too—and this is best of all—that *Plato and the Nerd* is written by a fellow nerd. He's one of *us*, a geek.

The Spark That Speaks Your Language

See if you, too, can make that spark—if indeed you find it speaking your language—yours for life. One way or another, remember to never give up on your search. *Ever*. One way or another, and hopefully *sooner* than later, you'll find your very own spark, waiting just for *you*...

Never give up on your search. One day, you'll find your very own spark; just keep your eyes peeled till then.

LETTER III: WOW, I WRITE

A Chimera,
Is merely that;
it's chimerical.
A leap of faith,
Is much more; it's a miracle.
Friends, please don't look at me askance—
Lean on my poetry, and may your words dance;
May they be lovely ritornellos that prance—
May they. Always.
I will hold your hands as you sing,
I'll sing your words with you;
Always.
- Akram Ahmad (Free—as in "uncaged"—verses by a
writer, blogger, software craftsman, son, husband, father,
brother, and friend)

Dear Reader,

With this letter, and more so than with the previous two, I wish to lift the veil that enshrouds the *joy* of writing so you, too, can be well on your way to writing down the bones. Put another way: Get ready (1) to dream, (2) to think anew like a child, (3) to get at the DNA itself of writing, among other things. As best as I can, I will try to lift the veil slowly, the better to avoid getting a case of the bends as deep sea divers sometimes do; and of you, I ask only that you approach the gentle advice which follow in the spirit of a bird that is being freed from a cage. Locked for far too long.

Let's begin with a sentiment expressed best by the inveterate sleuth Sherlock Holmes, shall we? It is my fond hope that after you've read this letter, you, too, will be inclined to say, "*Wow, I Write.*"

(Oh, and when you come to the dialog—the one between your writer-blogger and his (other) readers—which follows the sentiment I alluded to above, please pretend that I've never used the phrase "*didactic discourse*". Ever. Phrases such as this seemingly innocuous one—um, so that one was "*didactic discourse*"—have been known to stop otherwise phlegmatic and hardy souls in their tracks.)

> *How often have I said to you that when you have eliminated the impossible, whatever remains, however improbable, must be the truth?*
> *- Sir Arthur Conan Doyle (in the words of the enduring sleuth, Sherlock Holmes)*

As we near yet another scene, an animated dialog is taking place —between the readers of this blog—and we think twice about whether we ought to join the fray. We finally decide, gulp, to dive *right* into the fray.

First Reader: "Let me see if I got this right: This unrepentant blogger is back today with a *third* essay in this series?!"

Second Reader: "Looks like it."

Blogger [eavesdropping on the conversation]: "This sounds good. I sure like engaged readers, nothing like having legions of engaged readers now. Hmm... Their use of the adjective 'unrepentant', though, didn't quite sound all *that* complementary, come to think of it."

First Reader: "Oh. My. God."

Second Reader: "I can't believe it. Does he actually think that anyone is going to read a *third* essay when we were already done with his drivel, having barfed after several vain attempts to stomach his very *first* essay in the series. As for his *second* essay, oh well, it had sent some of us to the loo in fits of incontinence."

Blogger: "Hmm... This isn't sounding complementary *at* all. I wonder what *gives*?"

First Reader: "Yo, stop—*too* much information there, that talk of incontinence and all, you know!"

Second Reader: "Oops, sorry."

Blogger: "Surely they can't be talking there about the gems that are my essays, now *could* they. *Could* they?"

First Reader: "But you know what I'm saying, don't you?"

Second Reader: "I *do*."

Third Reader [joining the first two readers]: "*All* that this belligerent blogger's got is a boatload of bravado and banality"

Blogger: "Gulp!"

Chorus of Readers, *sans* **Blogger**: "Ho, ho, ho. These are the days of fixing-up the (Programming Digressions) blog—aye, and the blogger, too—for they surely *are*. Ho, ho, ho."

First Reader: "On the first day we got comatose drivel—*On Writing: Or Why I Write?*"

Second Reader: "On the second day, moribund trash—*On Writing: Or How I Write?*"

Third Reader: "And on the third day, *yet* more junk—*On Writing: Or, Wow I Write?*"

Blogger: "Double gulp!"

First Reader: "Oh. My. God."

Second Reader: "Where *is* that blogger? Let's find him and teach him a lesson, *shall* we?"

Third Reader: "Let's *do* it. But first, why don't we rally *more* troops and show up in numbers when we get a hold of the persnickety pest of a blogger?"

Blogger: "Triple gulp!"

First Reader: "Yeah."

Second Reader: "Oh *yeah*, for sure."

Third Reader: "Let's be done with the tarred banality this blogger keeps sending our way, *once* and for all—let's *do* it."

Blogger: "*I'm* outta here."

Oh well. Meanwhile, we get to hear other talk, this time actually a plaintive *plea*—for a pattern language—coming to you courtesy of a (somewhat) penitent purveyor of ideas: your blogger.

A Guide To The Fun We'll Be Having

We have some ground to cover here—albeit to a lesser degree than the previous two essays in this grand series—because this essay is all about the joy and gestalt of writing. So let's get started with a bird's eye view of the sojourns we'll hit during the upcoming excursion.

1. The Writer Is Never For Sale
2. The Cage Must Be Unlocked
3. Why Does A Writer Work So Hard?
4. Who Stops You From Dreaming?
5. What Havoc Could Writing Wreak?
6. The Writer Should Be Like A Child
7. Write For Those Who Love Books
8. Beware The Myths That Surround The Writer
9. Knead And Mold The Clay Of Words

So yeah, we have some ground to cover; not an overwhelming amount, but substantial enough to warrant your packing some gear for the journey.

Ready? Great! Let's jump right into the excursion.

A Pattern Language

Some Background

Having enjoyed working in the software trenches for over two
decades now—and getting a kick out of it every day I wake up

and go to work—I dream in software design patterns even when I'm *awake,* paradoxical as it sounds. Go figure.

Yep, you knew where this is going: an introduction of sorts to a pattern language in which I'm going to mold what follows. No doubt, the genesis of the notion of a pattern language inasmuch as it applies to software design—rest assured that I'll be introducing it shortly—can be traced back to the seminal book that rocked our industry a bit over two decades ago:

Design Patterns: Elements of ReuBut upsable Object-Oriented Software (Addison Wesley) by Gamma, E., R. Helm, R. Johnson, and J. Vlissides

And the *way* it rocked our software industry was right up there with a tsunami, albeit a benign one; a tsunami that *nourished* rather than demolished on whichever shores its waves crashed. In other words, it was a tide—albeit a massive one—that lifted all boats unlike any other that our industry had seen before.

Inspiration

As to what I offer to you today, should you wish to take it, my inspiration comes from *another* source. It's the one I cite below. In particular, my inspiration for marshaling a pattern language comes from a *discussion* of the aforementioned book (i.e. *Design Patterns*) in the pages of the gem that I now cite:

Plato and the Nerd: The Creative Partnership of Humans and Technology (The MIT Press) by Edward Ashford Lee

I hope you'll enjoy the feast that I've prepared for you. I welcome you to carve—nay, dissect—the "pieces" of the *feast* (it's not a *pie*, after all) along the lines of the pattern language that follows.

The Pattern Language: Annotated

Here, then, is the pattern language in which I've cast each of the nine pieces that make up the bulk of this essay:

Heading: A short description of what any given piece is about (Precisely so, yay!)
My two cents' worth: My editorial "wisdom" (You back there, stop snickering. Now!)
Quotation: A quotation to lend texture to the discussion (Playing with word-painting.)
Picture: A picture with which to ground the narrative (This will be your ticket.)
Poem: A poem to wrap it up into a unified whole (Big gifts do come in small packages at times.)

I Had Also Wished To...

I had wished, too, to talk some—though considerations of time and space interfere with that at the moment—about the misguided myth that writing is somehow painful; nothing could be farther from the truth.

Writing is *anything* but about pain. It is, truth be told, far closer to my imagination of the state of euphoria; and *then* some.

Yet, and much to my chagrin, that unsavory myth (about writing being a chore) persists. On top of that, I may have unwittingly *contributed* to it—though hopefully in only the *teensiest* way. I feel strongly about the utterly misguided notion that writing is somehow about pain; it positively is *not*. And to the extent that I haplessly *contributed* to that myth, I'm that much livid with myself.

Indeed, as memorably noted by the great Persian poet Omar Khayyám in his Rubáiyát, in the impeccable English translation by Edward Fitzgerald,

The Moving Finger writes; and, having writ,
Moves on: nor all thy Piety nor Wit
Shall lure it back to cancel half a Line,

Nor all thy Tears wash out a Word of it.

My fond wish, attached as it is to this letter, is that it'll go *some* way toward bringing the pristine, untarnished—and un-varnished—truth about the gestalt of writing out into the light of the sun for it to gleam in.

Just the other day, in fact, a friend was telling me just the other day that it's interesting how Omar Kyayyam—at least *during* his lifetime—was better known as an astronomer and a mathematician (than as the brilliant writer, which he also undeniably was.) What a polymath.

The Scoop

What I'm referring to above—in ruefully noting how I may have unwittingly contributed to the silly mystique that writing is a painful process—is my having quoted (groan, on *several* occasions) the following stark observation by George Orwell:

> *Writing a book is a horrible, exhausting struggle, like a long bout of some painful illness. One would never undertake such a thing if one were not driven on by some demon whom one can neither resist nor understand.*

Whenever I have quoted Orwell, as I did above, my only goal has been—nothing less and nothing more—to make the more vivid how I find myself resonating with the theme that the art of writing is *all* passion. It's about your inner writer (your writerly self) urging you to let *him* (or her) breathe and thereby live through *your* act of writing.

Please don't snuff out a life.

Promise me that you won't?

Extenuating Circumstances?

I suppose that the *one* extenuating circumstance that comes to mind is when—in quoting Orwell an umpteenth time in my essays—I had added an accompanying note (such as the following one from an earlier essay), reflecting on how

> *...I find myself resonating with this quote from George Orwell, though with nowhere near the acuteness which Orwell surely must have experienced when he divulged in "Why I Write" (England Your England and Other Essays)*

All I was trying to do there (by way of the fateful quotation above) was simply this: Underscore the elemental role of *passion* in writing. *Waah*, look what I ended up doing? (Helping perpetuate a myth.)

The Joy Of Writing

Look—*once* and for all, *plain* and simple—the art of writing is all about joy, compassion, and passion. Above all, writing is about being of service to others. If anyone tells me that writing is about money or something like that, I'm going to clobber them over the head.

Hey, hey, *hey*! Not to worry, though: I rattled off the "clobbering" image above *metaphorically* only—this is for all my literal-minded readers out there—to underscore how strongly I feel about this subject. Again, all that I said above (about "clobbering" and all) was in jest. Look, I'm decidedly pacifist. All good, then?

Interlude

What Colors My Writing. Evermore.

Having introduced a pattern language—with which to decipher and decode the pieces of writing gestalt that'll follow shortly—

allow me to remind you of the *real* source of my inspiration that colors much of everything I do nowadays as a writer.

I think you know what I'm talking about... Yes, I *thought* you did. As has been said, and very rightly so, that *"the price of liberty is eternal vigilance"*, it is equally true that *"the price of finding your spark is eternal writing"*; writing down the *bones*, in other words.

And Then The Words Ran Free

A confession first: My words have run free; at times I find myself drowning in the primordial ooze of creativity; imagine if you will how one simply *has* to rise to the surface ever so often lest one drown in the wondrous gifts with which creativity drenches—nay, submerges—the one who has found his or her muse.

Mind you, all that I said above, I said so unabashedly. At the same time, and paradoxically enough, I ask of you to <u>*forgive* me for some of the things that I say</u> for some of the things that I find myself saying nowadays. Speaking of which, much of what I just said might not have made sense to *you*; some of it still doesn't make sense to *me*.

What I've trying to do in this "Interlude" is, to the best of my abilities—and hopefully with a modicum of success—to share something of the *real* source of inspiration that fuels me as a writer.

I suppose—and there's truth to the adage that a picture is worth a thousand words—I wish now to complement the "word-painting" above with some good old "picture-painting.

How does that grab you? All good?

Great! Let's go.

A Tribute Of Sorts

So what I've next got for you is a tribute to the epicenter of my source of inspiration: It started out with the idea to arrange a bunch of books in a circle on the carpet in my living room—

with the inspirational epicenter square center of course—and take a picture of the tangible collage that I was going to prepare. I carried out the plan above. So where are the results? That's next.

The picture, which I snapped with my iPhone earlier this morning, is what you'll see below.

The Widening Gyre

What you're about to witness via the picture below can be thought of as just that, a mere *picture*; one writer's conceptualization of an embryonic *collage*, albeit one in gestation. Look, *however* you wish to look at it, I would like for you to please keep in your mind's eye the idea of how the sun lies at the center of our solar system. Our primary residence, our solar system, that is, complete with nine planets, including ours—planet Earth—circling around their source of energy (the sun) as they hurtle through space at enormous velocities.

Versailles (Actually, Verses) Of Rhyme

Now, as for the verses of rhyme that spontaneously came to my mind somewhere during a flash in the past 24 hours—which I later thought would nicely accompany the collage—I somehow managed to scribble those verses down. Yay!

As they say, and dare I say it's a Chinese proverb, that the *faintest* of inks is stronger than the *strongest* of memories. You'll find those verses of rhyme on the *other* side of the collage below.

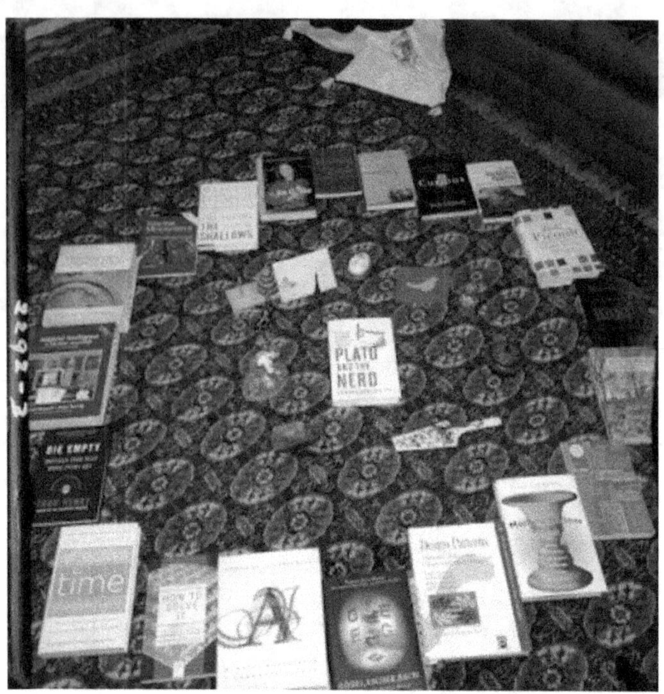

At the center of my universe, I see something lie,
Defying mortality, it will never, ever die; Written and
fueled in equal parts by intellect and heart,

It dwells in my mind from where it surely will never de-
part; Remember, as mortals, it's for us to live and die,
I embrace that truth, it's not for us to heave and sigh; Take
ashes away in a hearse or a cart or whatever plays the
part,

All I know are the souls by my side, who around in my vi-
sion dart; Poetic justice knows neither death nor will it on
anyone impose,
It remains at peace: calm and unruffled in its beatific re-
pose.
- Akram Ahmad (Rhymed verses by a writer, blogger,
software craftsman, son, husband, father, brother, and

friend)

At The Epicenter Was...

And there you have a star at the epicenter of my constellation—my super-special books of all time.

My verses are obviously ground zero, both literally *and* metaphorically. Why did I say that? Here's why: I used the word "metaphorically" because of the symbolism of the epicenter of a phenomenon and I used the word "literally" because of what I'm going to share next—writing greatness, the phenomenal Emily Dickinson whose poetry is light years more elevated than anything I could ever write in just as many light years.

Note, too, some hints of the undercurrents of the Dickinson poem that follows; there's more than a dash of how these verses of rhyme touch upon the centrality—think epicenter—of one's object of attention, of one's devotion. Thus it was that Dickinson had a story to tell of how

The soul selects her own society,
Then shuts the door;
On her divine majority
Obtrude no more.
- Emily Dickinson

Now, is that writing greatness or *is* that writing greatness?

With our brief foray into inspiration, writing, and writing greatness, we're now ready to finally dive into the essay *proper*.

(A brief look, if you will now thumb back a few pages to the section entitled "*The Pattern Language: Annotated*—made up of the elements that are "*Heading, My two cents' worth, Quotation, Picture,* and *Poem*"—will serve you well in the pages that follow.)

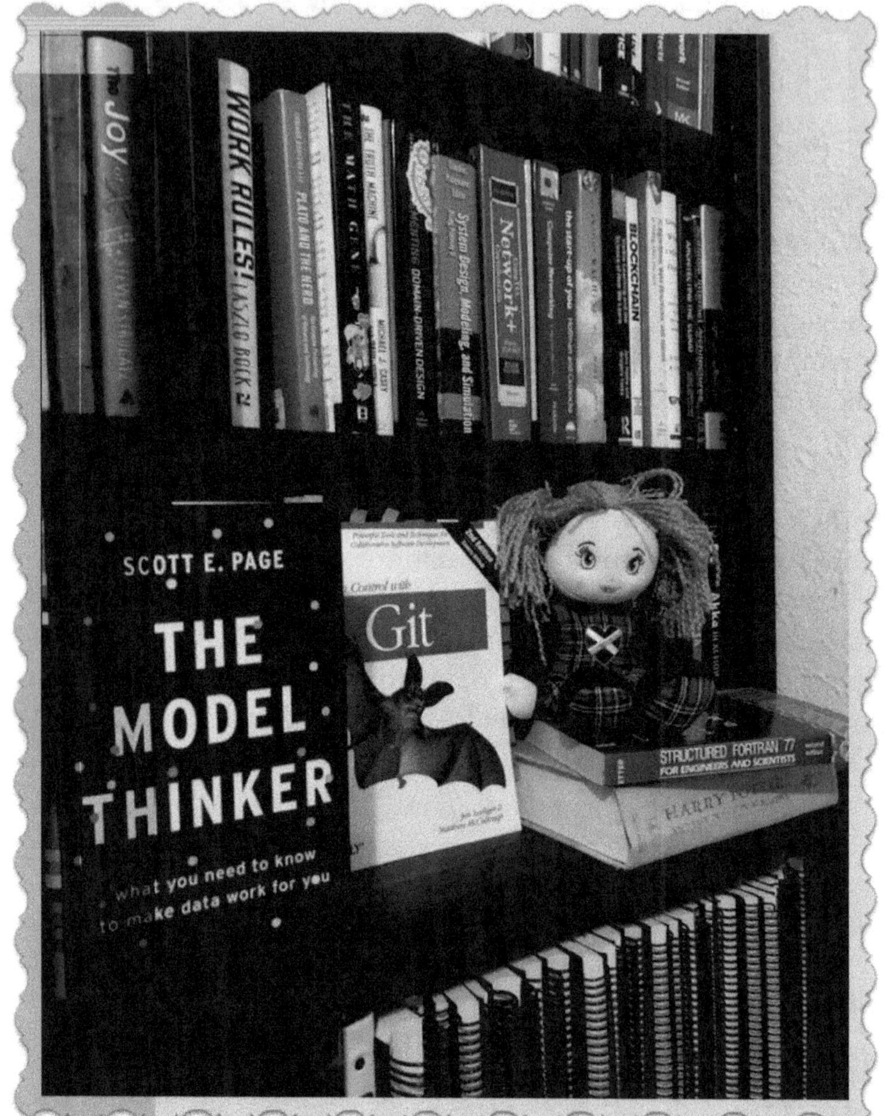

1. The Writer Is Never For Sale

My two cents' worth: Through her writings, a writer sticks her neck out, knowing full well that her neck may well get wrung. But she is brave; she *has* to be bold. I hope that suffices to demonstrate the writer is never for sale. Ever.

Perhaps you'd like to buy a flower?
But I could never sell.
If you would like to borrow
Until the daffodil.
- Emily Dickinson

2. The Cage Must Be Unlocked

My two cents' worth: The writer's personal experience—is there even such a thing as an "impersonal" experience?—cannot be discounted; it simply cannot. Experience, when shared the way it ought to be—provided that justice has been done to its delivery—is *way* too elemental a force to remain stoppable or be prevented from going viral.

All his thoughts were congealed into lines on his face, as the vapors
Freeze in fantastic shapes on the window-panes in the winter.
- Henry Wadsworth Longfellow

3. Why Does A Writer Work So Hard?

My two cents' worth: The writer works this hard for the same reasons that parents give of themselves so freely—utterly—to their children.

The writer of this legend then records
Its ghostly application in these words:
The image is the Adversary old,
Whose beckoning finger points to realms of gold
- Henry Wadsworth Longfellow

4. Who Stops You From Dreaming?

My two cents' worth: By way of a one-word answer—nobody. *Nobody* in the world but you has the right to decide your dreams for you. Nobody but you. Listen to your loved ones as you absolutely should; they care for you, they truly do. Listen, too, to your friends; they often mean well. But when it comes time to calling the shots on what you'll dream of, it's all on one individual: you.

Some men see things as they are and ask why. Others dream things that never were and ask why not.
- George Bernard Shaw

But the silence was unbroken, and the stillness gave no token,
And the only word there spoken was the whispered word, "Lenore!"
This I whispered, and an echo murmured back the word "Lenore!"
Merely this, and nothing more.
- Edgar Allan Poe (from his intense poem, The Raven)

5. What Havoc Could Writing Wreak?

My two cents' worth: Before you take the plunge into writing—and I encourage you to dive feet first into the waters of writing—do remember that only good things can happen. Enough said.

Soul, wilt thou toss again?
By just such a hazard
Hundreds have lost, indeed,
But tens have won an all.
- Emily Dickinson

6. The Writer Should Be Like A Child

My two cents' worth: If you wish to attain writing *goodness*, emulate the masters of writing; should you aspire to writing *greatness*, emulate children in what they do. On a regular basis. Every single day. No exceptions.

> *With a love that the winged seraphs of Heaven Coveted her and me.*
> *- Edgar Allan Poe (Annabel Lee)*

7. Write For Those Who Love Books

My two cents' worth: Write for yourself, and of course for those who love to read. Nothing less, nothing more, and you'll come out ahead.

> *I am a writer of books in retrospect. I talk in order to understand; I teach in order to learn.*

- Robert Frost

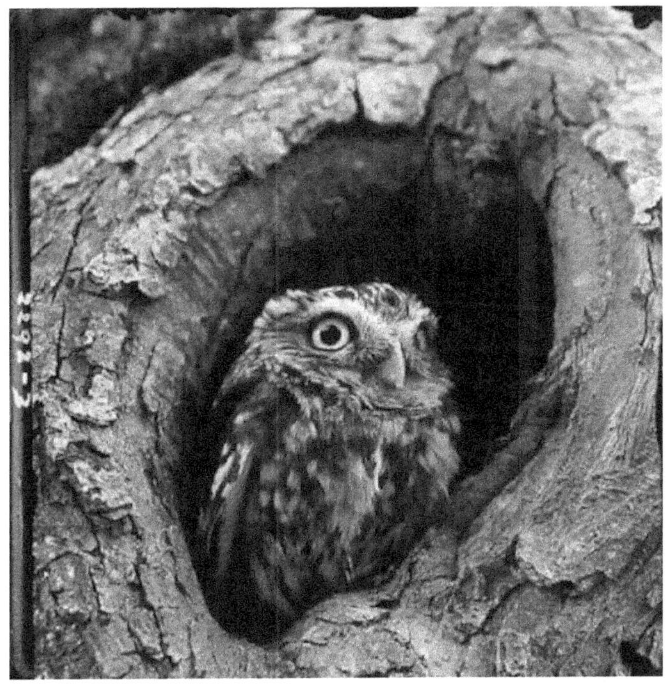

At evening when the lamp is lit,
Around the fire my parents sit;
They sit at home and talk and sing,
And do not play at anything.
- Robert Louis Stevenson

8. Beware The Myths That Surround The Writer

My two cents' worth: Here be dragons. Slay them or learn to *live* with your demons, at your own peril of course.

'Classic:' A book which people praise and don't read.
- Mark Twain

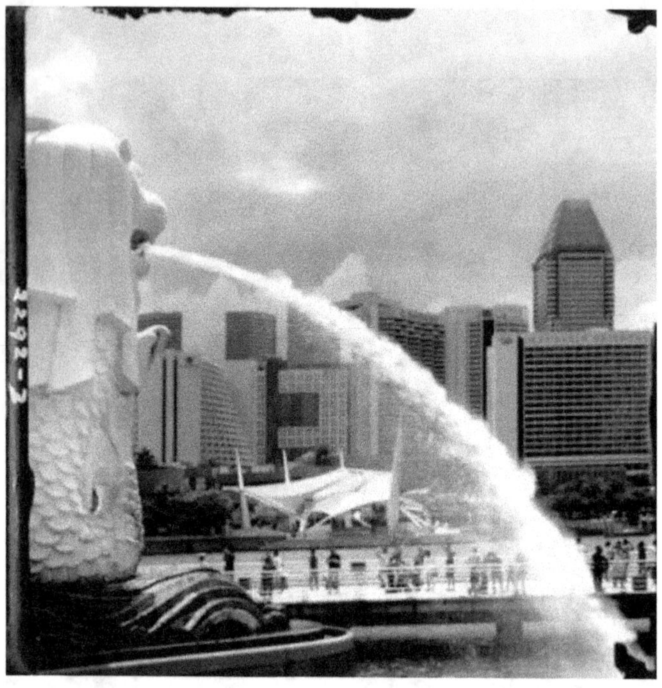

Miniver Cheevy, child of scorn,
Grew lean while he assailed the seasons;
He wept that he was ever born,
And he had reasons.
- Edwin Arlington Robinson (Miniver Cheevy)

9. Knead And Mold The Clay Of Words

My two cents' worth: Go out of your way to find out how Emily Dickinson writes. Your clay, the raw material with which you work—the words with which you paint your prose and poetry—may well get transmuted into birds that take flight, transfigured birds that soar heavenward.

Invention, it must be humbly admitted, does not consist

in creating out of a void, but out of chaos; the materials must in the first place be afforded; it can give form to dark, shapeless substances, but cannot bring into being the substance itself.
- Mary Shelley

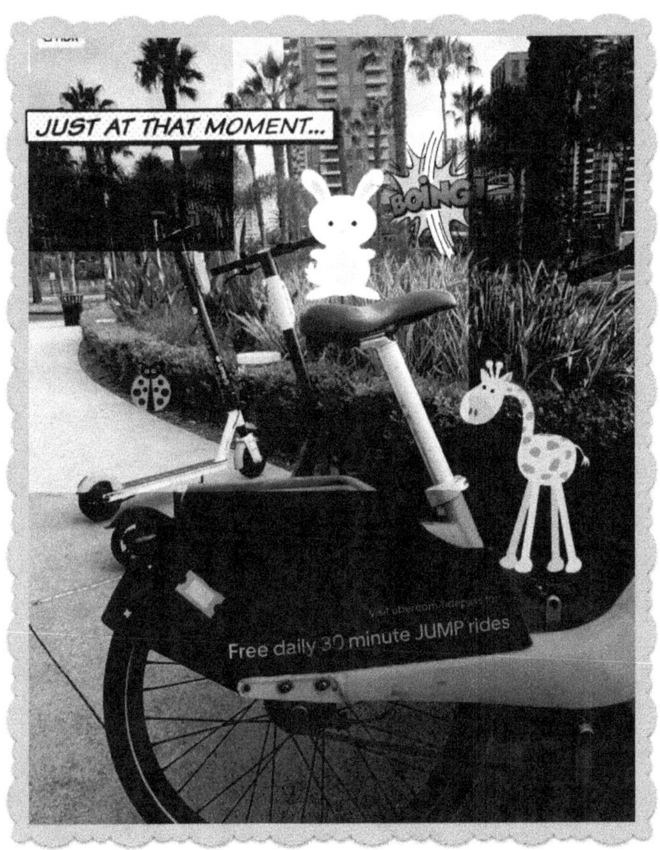

When figures show their royal front
And mists are carved away,—
Behold the atom I preferred
To all the lists of clay!
- Emily Dickinson

LETTER IV: NOW, I WRITE

Dear Reader,

We have come to our fourth letter, and I remain in the dark in matters pertaining to exactly *who* my benefactor is in delivering my letters to you... Is it the trusty staff at the post office in Candleford—of the TV series *Lark Rise to Candleford* fame—or is it our feathered friends the owls from the *Harry Potter* movies?

Either way, my chief concern is that these letters get safely delivered to your doorsteps.

On my end, here's what I got: More freewheeling than its brethren letters, this fourth one invites you to (1) become a chaser-of-ideas, (2) ride the unicorn of your imagination, (3) hitch your wagon to a star, among other things. And we're just getting *started*.

I say, though, that we start with some verses of *rhyme*—they just happen to be by yours truly—verses that were inspired by a writing virtuoso, the towering poet from yesteryear, Emily Dickinson, her poetry evergreen as ever. Here are my verses of rhyme:

> *So that was then; my life was mostly about reading... It just was, somehow,*
> *Then something happened: things changed and I; I mostly write now*

> *Yes, this is now; acres of books having been dutifully culled and harvested,*
> *Something lingered, though: the readings, of their meaning, had not been divested*

And of everything that I managed to digest,
Emily, your peerless poetry is simply the best

Your eloquence is the quintessence,
Of everything I aspire to in essence

You showed us how to make immortal sentences breathe
—in the first place, showed us indeed what they look like,
What you chiseled in crimson granite—liberating sen-
tences that would've otherwise suffocated—we have since
not seen their like

Loved ones who have left Earth, and whom we have un-
wittingly outlived,
Their mortality and their lives—in our minds—are indel-
ibly etched; limned

One by one—all of us on the face of Earth—we will perish,
but not the human soul,
Like your poetry, Emily, the soul has been vouchsafed to
remain inviolable; whole

So that was then, we sowed the seeds of reading; crops
grew, harvesting was done, and this is now
We are engulfed by fields of gold; the farmer hangs his hat,
and into the sunset walks the very last cow
- Akram Ahmad ("Lit", a random poem by a writer, blogger,
software craftsman, son, husband, father, brother, and
friend)

Preamble

As your callow blogger sits kneeling at the edge of a pond—
the full moon gleaming like a big white disc in the shimmering waters—he finds himself casting furtive glances at his own

image being reflected back... Evidently, some moments of reflection are afoot. Let's eavesdrop to find out what's up...

The (Dialogical-Enough) Dialog

Blogger [speaking to himself, soliloquy-style]: "Whatever happened to make my readers so disenchanted with my essays? Whatever, oh goodness, *whatever*?"

Blogger [now recalling the conversation which he had overheard taking place between a handful of his readers, and not *too* long ago either]

A Thought Balloon, or two, or three [Inserted here as the Blogger recalls that conversation, part of which was as follows]:

First Reader: "On the first day we got comatose drivel—On Writing: Or Why I Write?"

Second Reader: "On the second day, moribund trash—On Writing: Or How I Write?"

Third Reader: "And on the third day, *yet* more junk—On Writing: Or, Wow I Write?"

Blogger: "Gulp. And here I am, contemplating the submission of a new essay to tack on to that series of essays, one which I'm going to call *On Writing: Or Now I Write*"

[**Visualize this**: Unbeknownst to the Blogger—as he continued to ruefully glance at his somber reflection being cast in the shimmering waters—a handful of his readers had stealthily crept up to the edge of the pond where he sat kneeling. They were listening to every word of his soliloquy...]

First Reader: "Oh. My. God."

Second Reader: "Did you, like, *hear* what the Blogger just said?"

Third Reader: "Aye, we did... So we had never got around to rallying more troops and showing up in numbers when we had contemplated getting a hold of this persnickety pest of a blogger, and teaching him a lesson."

First Reader: "Yeah, *now* is our chance. Let's use the element of surprise and waylay him *real* good. Yeah!"

Second Reader: "Right. I mean, did you, like, follow what he

[Blogger] just said?"

Third Reader: "Right, right... He plans on sending yet another trashy essay our way—the misguided soul wants to call this one *On Writing: Or Now I Write*, or something if I heard him right."

First Reader: "Yeah, let's fix up this persnickety pest, shall we?"

Second Reader: "Right. Let's do it before this irascible urchin writes up even *more* trash."

Third Reader: "*Exactically!* Ahem, I mean *exactly*... Dude, looks like he's going for it! This blogger's got *yet* another garbage essay—this one called, like you said *On Writing: Or Now I Write* up his sleeve, if I, too, heard him right."

First Reader: "Yeah, let's fix him up real, *real* good this time!"

Second Reader: "Oh yeah! Next thing you know, he'll write up something even more outlandish and call it something like *On Writing: Or Kapow I Write*."

Third Reader: "Oh no he won't. We'll make his next essay—*should* he dare to write another one—sound mournful all right, something like... *On Writing: Ow Ow I Had Dared To Write*."

Blogger [still speaking to himself, soliloquy-style—goodness, it's rightly been said that ignorance is bliss]: "To be, or not to be... Whoah! What's *going* on here? Egads! I'm overcome by... Prose Ruffians!"

Omitting a bunch of painful happenings that ensue next: a melee.

A Guide To The Fun Which Lies Ahead

We have some ground to cover here—albeit to a *lesser* degree than the previous *three* essays in this grand series—because this essay is *all* about the sweet joy and gestalt of writing.

Pit Stops (Aka Sojourns) On Our Journey

So let's get started with a bird's eye view of the sojourns we'll hit during the upcoming excursion ☐

    1. *Rewrite* Down The Bones

2. Become A Chaser-of-Ideas
3. Ride The Unicorn Of Your Imagination
4. Ponder On How Art Follows Life
5. Hitch Your (Writing) Wagon To A Star
6. Sprinkle Your Writing With The Pixie Dust Of (Kaleidoscopic) Music
7. Lose Yourself In The Immortal Quest For True Art (In Writing)
8. Write With The *Abundance* Of Devotion
9. Write With Valor: No Guts, No Glory

Receding Like The Distant Ship Smoke On The Horizon

Okay, so what you see above is the itinerary for the sojourns receding from us—excuse me there, I had meant to say—<u>*coming our way*</u>: So I wasn't joking when I noted above that we have *some* ground to cover; not anywhere near what we had in the past couple of essays, but *substantial* enough, nonetheless, to warrant your packing at least *some* gear for the journey ahead. Ready? Got that trusty backpack slung across your shoulder? Great, let's start our journey with that crucial first step.

A Pattern Language

Brief Background

Much as I had said in the last essay, having enjoyed working in the trenches of software design and development for over two decades now—and getting a kick out of it every single day still when I wake up and launch into my work—I dream in software design patterns *even* when I'm awake. Is that paradoxical or what? *You* go figure that one out; *I've* already got a boatload of metaphysics on my hands.
Yep, you knew where this is going, don't you? So we're veer-

ing toward an introduction of sorts to a pattern language, that being the language in which I'm going to mold and dissect—nay, gently vivisect—all that which will follow the intro...

Still got those hoary geometry boxes from your high school days around? *Now* would be a good time to rummage for them, brush off the funk of forty thousand years deposited on their crusty exterior, and...

Ow, ow! Stop jabbing me. Hey, I give up; you're not *that* old. I was just kidding about your wizened look. In fact, methinks you're not old *at* all.

Ahem, no doubt, the genesis of the notion of a pattern language, inasmuch as it applies to software design—rest assured that I'll be introducing it shortly—can be traced back to the seminal book that rocked our industry a bit over two decades ago:

Design Patterns: Elements of Reusable Object-Oriented Software (Addison Wesley) by Gamma, E., R. Helm, R. Johnson, and J. Vlissides

And the *way* it rocked our software industry was right up there with a tsunami, albeit a benign one; a tsunami that *nourished* rather than demolished on whichever shores its waves crashed. In other words, it was a rising tide—albeit a massive one—that had lifted all boats unlike any other that our industry had seen before.

The Pattern Language: Annotated

Here, then, is the pattern language in which I've cast each of the nine pieces (the nine pit stops) that make up the bulk of this essay:

Heading: *A short description of what any given piece is about (Precisely so, yay!)*
My two cents' worth: *My editorial "wisdom" (You back*

there, stop snickering. Now!)
Quotation: *A quotation to lend texture to the discussion (We play with word-painting.)*
Picture: *A picture with which to ground the narrative (This will be your ticket.)*
Poem: *A poem to wrap it all up into a unified whole (Big gifts can come in small packages.)*

In the end, I hope you will agree that there *is* a method to this (pattern language-inspired) madness.

Revisiting A Theme...

So I wish to talk some—though considerations of time and space forever seem to interfere with this particular goal of mine —about the utterly misguided notion that writing is somehow painful; *nothing* could be farther from the truth.

Much as I've said elsewhere, writing is *anything* but about pain. It is, truth be told, far closer to everything that I could've ever imagined the state of euphoria to be; and *then* some.

If you look for one recurring theme in this essay, I sure hope it will be this one: writing is all about joy, sharing, caring, and daring. Yes, writing is *also* about passion. It surely is. But writing has nothing to do with pain. Nothing *whatsoever*! Yes, that's how strongly I feel about this subject.

With that, we're now finally ready to dive into the essay *proper*. Having said that—"that what follows next is the essay *proper*"— does not, by the same token, relegate what came earlier to a state of being *improper*. At least I *hope* not.

1. Rewrite Down The Bones

My two cents' worth: Yet another recurring theme pervades the writing life… If I could point to an especially pervasive theme permeating the writer's life, my finger would point in this direction: writing is all about *rewriting*. Think James Michener.

Going to him! Happy letter! Tell him—
Tell him the page I didn't write;
Tell him I only said the syntax,
And left the verb and the pronoun out.
- Emily Dickinson

2. Become A Chaser-of-Ideas

My two cents' worth: Be on the lookout for ideas like the surfer lying in wait for the perfect wave to crest and pounce on—surfboard and all—riding it to glorious joy. You will, of course, weave a narrative out of those ideas, crafting an essay, a memoir, a story, or whatever you wish to. Or perhaps be like the anglers along the edge of a pond, eagerly poised with rod and reel in hand, seeing what you can fish out from what lies *without*, or—when so moved by the mood of contemplation—what lies *within*. In that there is no sin; you will hopefully fish out lots of ideas, and maybe even a fish fin.

There are thousands of thoughts lying within a man that
he does not know till he takes up the pen and writes.
- William Makepeace Thackeray

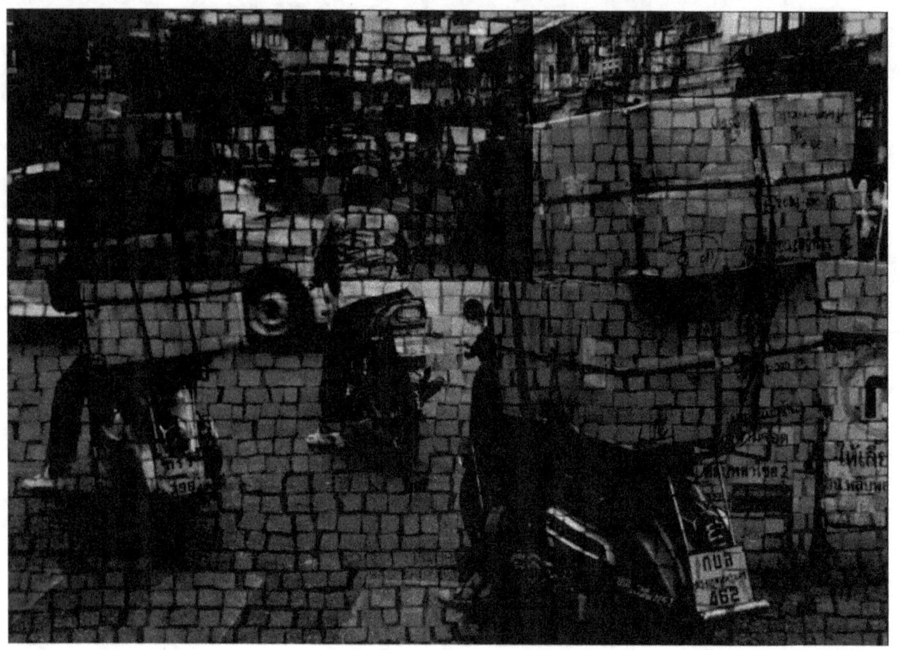

3. Ride The Unicorn Of
Your Imagination

My two cents' worth: There is freedom within, there is freedom without, try to catch the deluge in a paper cup... Torrents of creativity within, torrents of creativity without, it's all waiting there for you. Yes, *you.*

> *Most writers regard the truth as their most valuable possession, and therefore are most economical in its use.*
> *- Mark Twain*

> *Only in men's imagination does every truth find an effective and undeniable existence. Imagination, not invention, is the supreme master of art as of life.*
> *- Joseph Conrad*

4. Ponder On How Art Follows Life

My two cents' worth: I can but speak for myself in saying—much as I've said in an earlier essay—that I cannot n*ot* write. It is not pain that compels me to write; it is joy that does. It's not breathing which leads me to write; it's the urgency to avoid suffocation that does. At the end of the day, all such considerations—whether life follow art or art follows life—may come down to semantic hair-splitting. What matters is simply this: the world needs to see your art; please don't keep them waiting much longer, okay?

> *How vain it is to sit down to write if you have not stood up to live.*
> *- Henry David Thoreau*

5. Hitch Your (Writing) Wagon To A Star

My two cents' worth: Things which are both important and urgent always seem to get our full attention; things that are important but not urgent, on the other hand, seem to ever fall by the wayside. You have to change that because that's not how a writer lives her life. Gaze heavenward, would you please? Find the most beautiful star that gets your fancy… Hitch your wagon to that star and you'll be *all* good!

> *The writer must believe that what he is doing is the most important thing in the world. And he must hold to this illusion even when he knows it is not true.*
> *- John Steinbeck*

Each life converges to some centre

Expressed or still;
Exists in every human nature
A goal,
- Emily Dickinson

6. Sprinkle Your Writing With The Pixie Dust Of (Kaleidoscopic) Music

My two cents' worth: Some are born with it, some without. If you are in the former camp, rejoice. Remember, too, that you owe it to yourself—more importantly, you owe it to the *world* —to *share* your gift of writing in all its glory. Think noblesse oblige. And should you find yourself in the latter camp (and I'm right there with you), take heart: writing is an eminently learnable skill. We are all in this together, so read on...

Writing has laws of perspective, of light and shade, just as painting does, or music. If you are born knowing them, fine. If not, learn them. Then rearrange the rules to suit yourself.
- Truman Capote

From breakfast on through all the day
At home among my friends I stay, But every night I go abroad
Afar into the land of Nod.
- Robert Louis Stevenson

7. Lose Yourself In The Immortal Quest For True Art (In Writing)

My two cents' worth: It all comes down to this: In your *losing* yourself lies your victory. Be *selfless* as you immerse yourself in the search for true grace. Wield the pen and put it to paper to serve others; true art is *selfless*, infinitely deep in compassion, and immeasurably warm in reception. My promise to you all is but this: I will write down the bones. I will weep till my tears drench the words I write, in the hope that the moisture will revive those words and make them sing. *Should* you find melody in what you read here, *please* pass it along so that others—and I know that thousands out there lead lives of quiet desperation—can also take comfort in the knowledge that if an unknown like your blogger can make prose sing, so can *anyone*. Yes, anyone.

Once and for all, I want to obliterate the myth that writing is somehow reserved for some highfalutin writing priesthood. It simply is not. Writing is for all of us. Yes, including *us* commoners. For crying out loud, it's in our DNA. Don't you let anyone convince you otherwise, okay?

Art is a lie that makes us realize the truth.
- Pablo Picasso

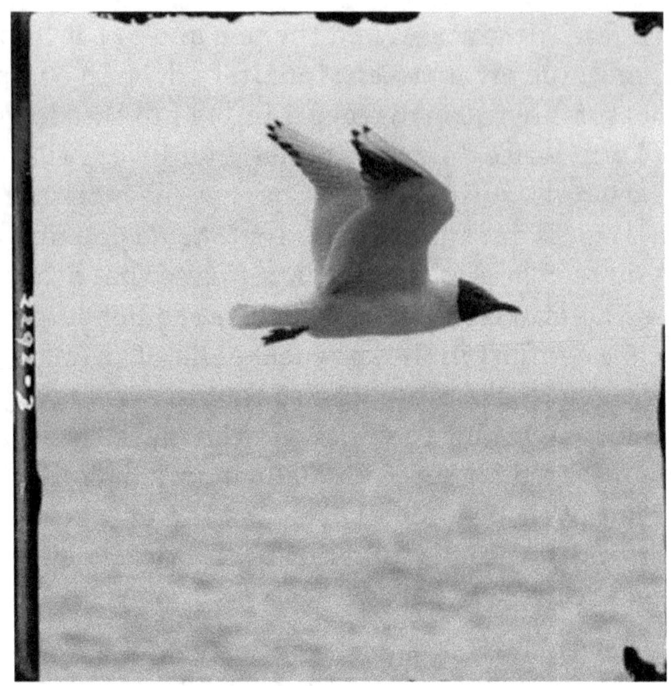

Healed by the touch of that hand, and he said, with a voice full of feeling:
"Yes, we must ever be friends; and of all who offer you friendship
Let me be ever the first, the truest, the nearest and dearest!"
- Henry Wadsworth Longfellow

8. Write With The Abundance Of Devotion

My two cents' worth: Even if you forget everything else that I have said up to this point, remember this: writing is not about money; it is not about fame; it's all about putting the abundance of your devotion to the service of your readers. Money and fame are but baubles and trinkets; Dave will never be the source of true satisfaction. Service to others is. Write prose to serve *others*. Of course, take joy and pride in what you do.

It is advantageous to an author that his book should be attacked as well as praised. Fame is a shuttlecock. If it be struck at one end of the room, it will soon fall to the ground. To keep it up, it must be struck at both ends.
- Samuel Johnson

Superfluous were the sun
When excellence is dead;
He were superfluous every day,
For every day is said
- Emily Dickinson

9. Write With Valor: No Guts, No Glory

My two cents' worth: Insipid writing does not leap from the page because it hasn't yet been animated by the spark of your imagination. It just lies there, moribund, curled up like lethargic looms of fog in the streets of London town at midnight. But that will not be *your* writing. You will write fearlessly; there is none to stop you. *Should* anyone demur, would you politely inform them that they will have to go through *me*? Yes, they will have to go through your blogger. Thank you.

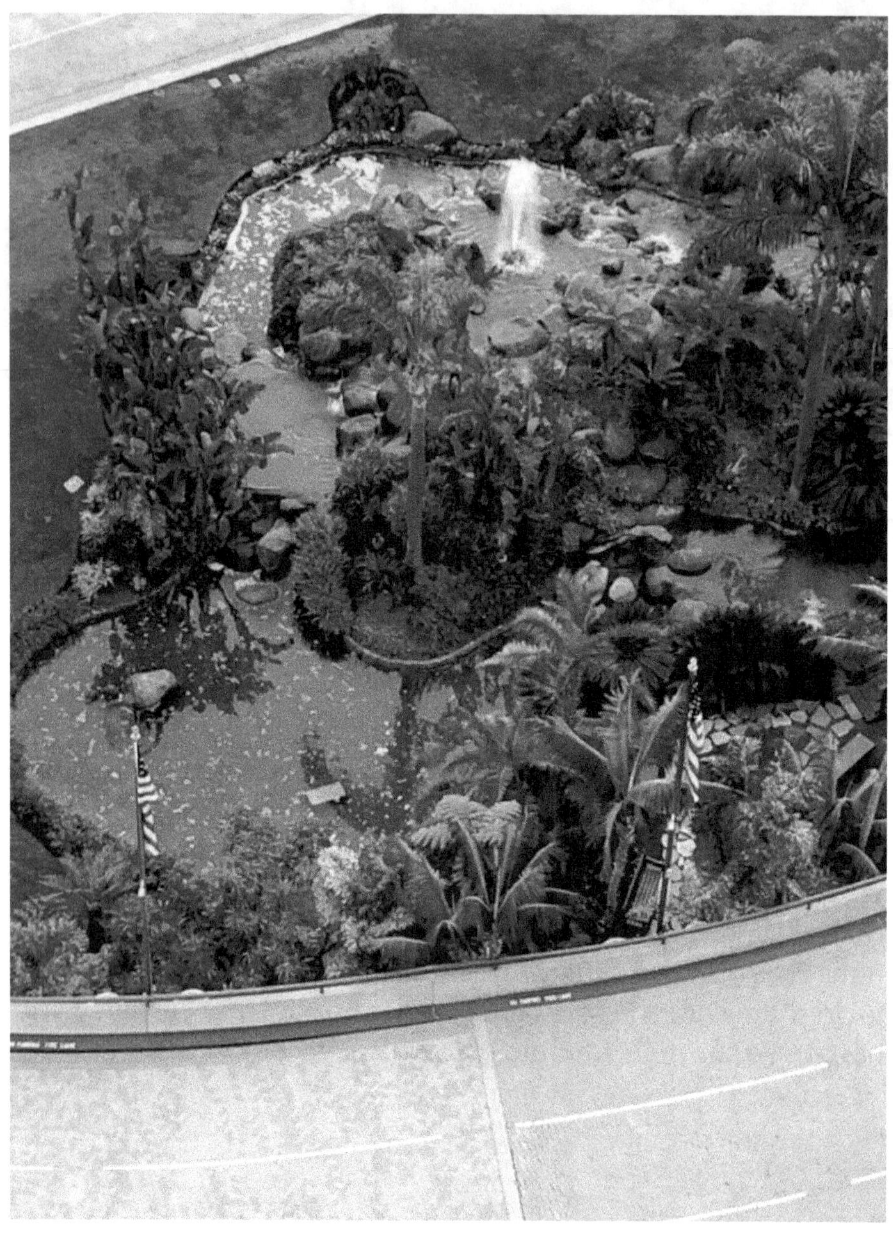

Epilogue

A Collage Reappears

As I was writing this essay, I shared an early draft with a dear friend (my brother, in fact) who pointed out something intriguing: In his beautifully wrought description (and he was referring to the picture of the *collage* <u>which had appeared in the *previous* essay</u>), he said in part that, "...it [the *collage*] recognizes the deep intellectual heritage that any piece of writing has..."

By the way, I touched up that *collage* with some admittedly jaundiced arrows—as it appears above—to better bring out the inter-connectedness of it all: how all that we read and write *today* is linked to all that we've read and written *before.* Now is that tenderness or is that nostalgia or is that...

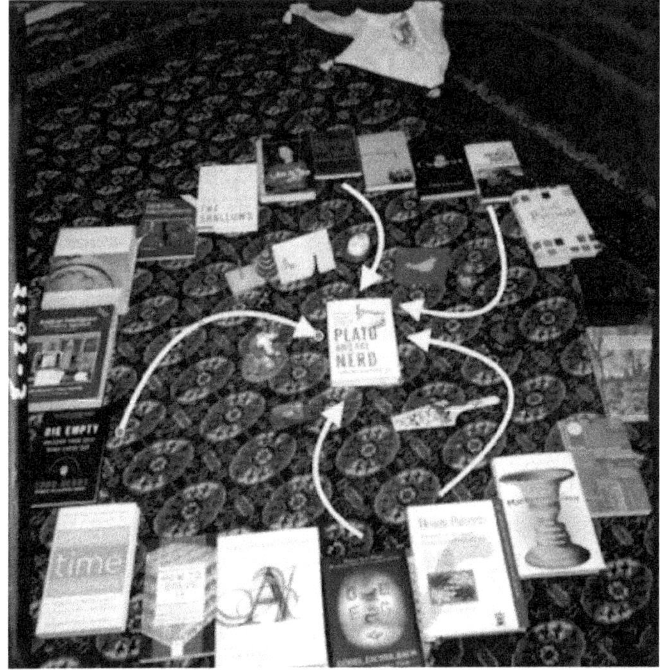

And yes, I found myself in full agreement with my brother's assessment: everything that I know, and will ever come to know, will—much as it already has—lean on someone else's work that came before. It surely has; it surely will, just as surely as the day follows the night.

It's Only Together That We Can Make It Happen!

As a matter of fact, I lean on *you*, my reader, to keep me educated and informed. So you all, don't you be shy. Please allow yourself to feel emboldened in sharing your thoughts via the comments which you will (surely) be posting here, and elsewhere, on other essays which have appeared previously in this blog (Programming Digressions.)

The (Latest) John Mcphee Book

Oh, to complete the thought above—recognizing the deep intellectual heritage that any piece of writing has—my brother pointed me in the direction of the new John McPhee book entitled *Draft No. 4: On the Writing Process*. There appears in McPhee's *Draft No. 4* a marvelous illustration of "Xs and Os", he pointed out, which is symbolism-writ-large of the structural aspects of the writing process.

So I grabbed my own copy of McPhee's *Draft No. 4*—I started reading it fairly recently, along with Isaacson's big new biography of Leonardo da Vinci—and sure enough, there it was: the deliciously congruent vivification of the structural aspects of the writing process, those naughty "Xs and O.s

A Parting Thought...

The only other thing I wish to add is this: When it comes to advice on writing style, or the writing process in general, most all the writing that I do—notwithstanding Professor Trimble's inimitable book on the subject as my trusty guide—and in fact most all the writing that I've done to date, I just "wing it."

Yep, I've been totally winging it: Obviously, the results—the essays that you read here—speak for themselves, wingdings and all.

LETTER V: A ROW WITH HOW I WRITE

*She had lost the art of conversation, but not, unfortu-
nately, the power of speech.*
- George Bernard Shaw

Dear Reader,

With this the fifth letter, I want to pause and utter a prayer that you do not find yourself thinking of me with the selfsame sentiment that Shaw expressed in his words above; I can only hope.

If you're still with me, check this before you start reading it: This letter, more so than the rest of its ilk, happens to be totally off-the-wall in that it dives deeper and deeper still into the writerly wisdom of a rather famous writing maven that is Stephen King.

Know, too, that I'm not into the horror genre at all. Never was, probably never will be. It's just that King's superb book (on the art of writing) knocked my socks off: Everyting that comes next in this the fifth letter to you had the maven writer's advice on writing serve as its springboard.

Shall we dive in?

Ember by ember, bit by bit,
Things warmed up, the fire was lit
Seared in the pit,

The words were writ

Bit by bit
Wit by wit
Slowly, mitt by mitt,

The essays were knit
Bit by bit,
Fit by fit
Essays saved and archived, hit by hit,
Pushed to Git, commit by commit

Missives undelivered or intercepted, chit by chit
So who subjugated who, Brit by Brit?
Brick upon brick, grit by grit,
The gleaming edifice was built

The rocket was readied for takeoff, bit by bit
The literature was assembled, DIY-kit by DIY-kit
Aha, this must be the house that Peterbilt,
Wait! No! This is the house that Akram built

Don Quixote sure had at the windmill, tilt by tilt,
So did Milton in his own way, I suppose "Milt" by "Milt"
So let the bits fly, Akram, you twit
Let 'em fly (like a snitch), wit by wit
Bit by bit,
Lit by lit

All the world's but a stage, with men and women engaged
in some bizarre skit,
*Where tweets alight from the sky like bird-poop, aerial s**t*
*by aerial s**t*
What is this thing with feathers that seems to dart about
and flit?,
Builds our dreams, yet goes for the throat, slit by slit

All the same, hit by hit,

The essays became fit
Every single essay I ever wrote, I winged it,
Every song that arose in my heart, I singed it

Ember unto ember, hilt unto hilt,
The embers glowed, the fire had been lit
Sit back and watch the embers show their glow; sit now sit,
Bask in the glowing edifice that's been rewrit; it's been lit.
- Akram Ahmad ("Ember by Ember" — another random poem by a writer, blogger, software craftsman, son, husband, father, brother, and friend)

The Definitions

1. **row** (noun): a noisy quarrel or dispute (Pronounced so as to rhyme with, um, "pow")

2. **daguerreotype** (noun): (a picture made by) an obsolete photographic process, invented in 1839, in which a picture made on a silver surface sensitized with iodine was developed by exposure to mercury vapor.

A Harbinger Of Things To Come

Grappling With A (Hitherto) Latent Journey

I would like to share with you—take you along with me, in fact—on a journey of sorts.

So I have lately been reckoning with certain themes, not at one level but two (the *micro* and the *macro*), just to make things more interesting:

Micro-cosmic: The first theme touches on an internal de-

bate, almost a quarrel—hence my use of the word "row" in the name of this essay—about how to reorient myself in my writing style to serve you better. This is about the ever-evolving writing style that I bring to the essays you read.

Macro-cosmic: As for the second theme, it's tinged by the yearning for a search, one fueled by magic: You know how sometimes we are looking for things and all the while we're not even aware of the deep yearning to find what was lost or maybe not even ours to begin with; yep, these are telltale signs of confabulation writ large in a discursive foray into dissimulation. Hey, something like that, anyway!

Good enough? Great, let's get going! (Not to worry; *no* New Age hand-waving going on either above or in what follows.)

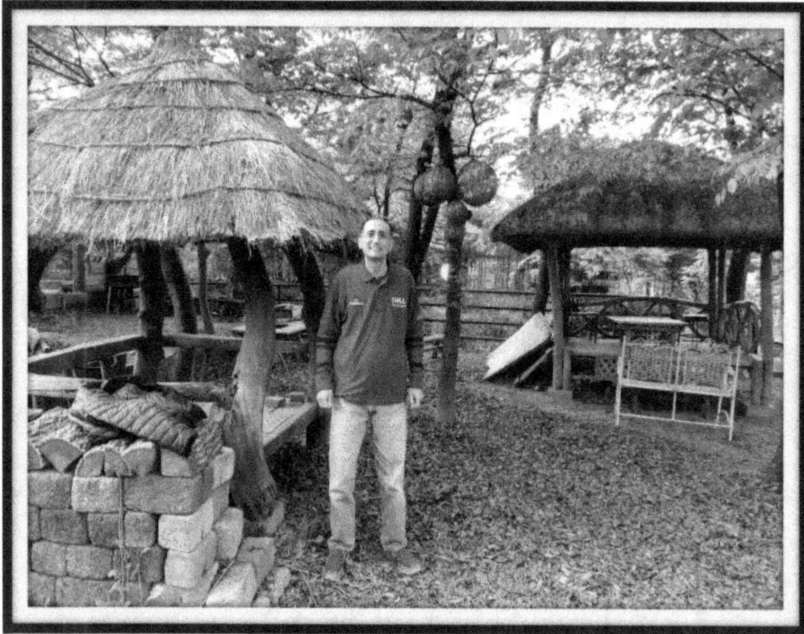

Your Blogger Is Awestruck

I was petrified as I read the book. Yes, petrified, *and* terrified: I was unnerved as I turned its pages, riveted—more like trans-fixed—by the story which the author was telling!

I felt terrified because I was witnessing phenomenal writing talent on display, a talent raw *yet* immensely well-trained at the same time, feral *yet* phenomenally-tamed at the same time; writing talent quite unlike anything I had seen before. If anyone remembers the classic movie *Chariots of Fire*: It's like when Harold Abraham, watching the 400 meters dash from the bleachers, clenches the paper flyer—which has the schedule of the races for the day—into a crumpled ball in his big fist as he witnesses the ferocity with which Eric Liddell runs, *and* wins, the race!

And I felt unnerved because I could scarcely believe that anyone could write with such conviction, with such clarity, with such passion; this was writing magnificence writ large.

Oh. My. God.

Clearly, I was moved by the book's message on an approach to the craft of writing, made all the more memorable by the riveting prose in which it was delivered.

This coming from a fan boy of Professor John Trimble's inimitable gem entitled *Writing with Style: Conversations on the Art of Writing*—long-time readers know full well that I fondly refer to that gem simply by its initials, *WWS*—*and* which I've asked of you (in the past) to commit to memory. No doubt, WWS came first and it will never be supplanted. All the same, the new book I'm raving about is a rather special bird; it's not a bird-by-bird chronicle—awesome though that chronicle is in its own right—but a unique bird all right.

So I surreptitious kept turning its pages, all the while telling myself that the magic that was engulfing me—leaping out at me as it was from the pages of this new book—was bound to wear off in a few pages. But that was not to be, I am delighted to report! The magic in the writing was showing no signs of wearing off: woohoo! And I kept reading, transfixed by what I was reading. Yay!

Unnerved by the ferocity of the writing, I kept turning its pages; it was the kind of rawness with which *I* want to write.

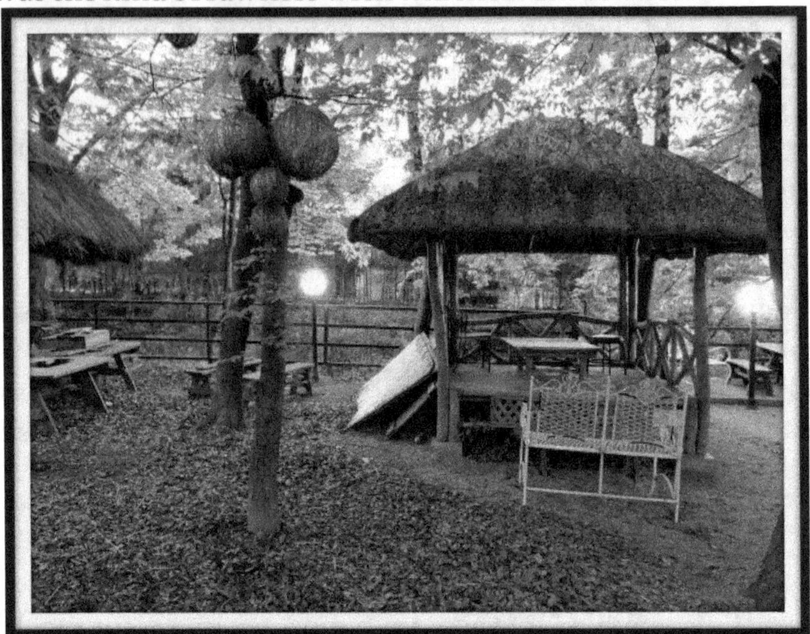

A Book On Writing Which...

...itself is a remarkable example of riveting prose. How about that?

The riveting prose in the new page-turner knocked my socks off; it was the kind of prose that *I* had always wanted to be able to write. Not only was I reading a master lesson in the craft of writing, I was also reading a sterling example of masterful writing from a writer at the peak of his career.

Here, then, was a book that practiced what it preached: delivering the message in harmony with its goals by serving as an excellent example itself of what riveting prose can look like. Yep, the whole notion of leading by example. Or to use an analogy from computer science—imprecisely so, by my own admission—here, then, was a book that could rightly claim to be an exegesis of the metacircular interpreter (which, in a nutshell, defines each feature of the interpreted language using a similar facility of the interpreter's host language.)

Had I Finally Met My Implacable Nemesis?

I had met my implacable nemesis; the kind of spur with which to leaven—not goad, mind you, but *leaven*—my overvaulting ambition to write like nobody in the world has written before. Before I get a million comments accusing me of having let all this writing go to my head, allow me to add (parenthetically) that writers do not compete with one another; we compete with ourselves. It's a meritocracy of one: *E pluribus unum.*

Then again, allow me to drive the point home that I'm not some arrogant prissy—people who know me have a *slightly* loftier view of me, at least they did, last time I checked what people have been writing about me. Anyhow, *all* that I had in mind in what I said above—"to write like nobody in the world has written before"—is wholly informed (neither more nor less) by the advice to

> *Be yourself; everyone else is already taken.*
> *- Oscar Wilde*

Cool?
Relax. We're all geeks and stuff over here, proletarians at heart (neither more nor less.)

Having Made My Case...

All the same, I've made the case: Should anyone catch me wringing my hands in the fashion of Lady Macbeth's hand-washing—look, did anyone ever catch me saying: *Out, damned spot?*—we can certainly chat more at that time. *Till* then, I bide my time. Tick, tock... More fashionably, think the hourglass: yep, these sure are the days of our lives.
Anyhow, *anyhow...*

The more I read my newly-discovered prize-of-a-book, the more I was convinced that I was beholding writing greatness; the more I dug into the captivating narrative, the more I was drawn in—deeper by the sentence, by the paragraph, by the chapter—increasingly assured that this was *not* a fluke.

The more I turned the pages of the book, the more I was impressed. I was witnessing writing awesomeness: clean, unencumbered, and unaffected prose that purred to me (Insert one "meow" here.)

Writing Awesomeness

I felt as if I was in the presence of awesomeness that was at once benevolent *and* didactic.

Loved it

On Writing: A Memoir of the Craft by Stephen King (Scribner, 10th Anniversary edition)

This is greatness to which I aspire, notwithstanding that I've fondly been called a *sprezzatura* by well-wishers; more on that million dollar word (*sprezzatura*) later, so not to worry (Till recently, I, too, didn't have a clue *either* as to what that word meant—it sure *sounds* like the name of a carbonated drink now, doesn't it?—until some events unfolded over the past several months.)

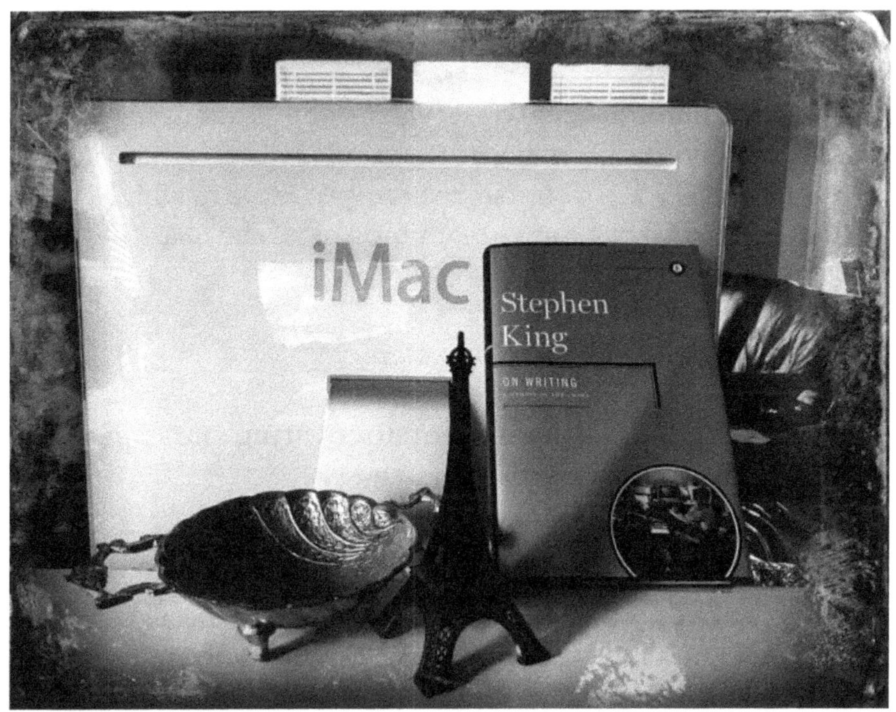

Life imitates art far more than art imitates Life.
- Oscar Wilde

So You've Found Your Spark: What Do We Do Next?

Something Of Themes & Memes

Lately, the theme foremost in my mind has been: What do you *after* you have discovered your spark, after you've discovered your muse? Indeed, what *do* you do? Do you wring your hands in despair and wait for inspiration to strike? I'm not a fatalist—*far* from it, I'm a *card*-carrying member of the (apocryphal?) alive pragmatists society—so that strategy (if fatalism can be glorified by calling it a "strategy") wasn't going to fly: no way, José. Or do I jump over a cliff like lemmings do? Nope, *way* too painful: uh-uh.

Oh, so in my parenthetical observation above about my having discovered my spark—many of my regular readers likely are *already* on to it—I was, of course, referring to the gem which got its very own handful of essays on our blog here, the *following* three to be precise:

- Plato And The Nerd
- Return of Plato And The Nerd
- Plato And The Nerd Strikes Back

I was also—in making mention of discovering one's muse—referring to someone I revere, someone

Anyhow... Yes, while I do of course freely share with you all the themes currently on my mind, sometimes even to the point of stream-of-consciousness narrative—look, you all are simply the best, I *love* you all—one can divulge only *so* much. So whether one's life should be considered an open book will remain an open question: fair enough?

Your Vienna Waits For You

Basically, having discovered your spark and found your muse, you go about <u>whichever way you can</u> to hone your writing skills. You knew where this was going, didn't you?
One more time, how *do* you get to Carnegie Hall?

Practice, practice, practice!

Much like computer programming—at least <u>the way *I* see it</u>—writing is *not* a spectator sport. You learn (and improve) by doing, *not* by merely watching (I firmly believe in the criticality of mentoring, which is basically showing-others-how-things-are-done, so don't get me wrong). At any rate, the analog (of the take above on getting to Carnegie Hall) in the writing world might be something like

One more time, how *do* you get your very own Pulitzer Prize?

Write, write, write!

The Scoop

Here's the deal: some are born *with* those skills, and some *without.* In full candor, your blogger finds himself squarely in the latter camp. Curiously enough, though, some have tried to convince me otherwise; that I'm actually in the *former* camp even as I remain firmly unconvinced by their kind conviction, incredibly kind—even humbling—and deeply appreciated though their gestures truly are.

You all, do please remind me to chat some about the time when I was moved to grab my copy of the new John McPhee book entitled *Draft No. 4: On the Writing Process.* In passing, here's the scoop: So I had grabbed my copy of McPhee's *Draft No. 4*— I had begun reading it fairly recently, not too long after diving into Isaacson's big new biography of Leonardo da Vinci—and couldn't help but get a kick out of McPhee's own run in with the whole *sprezzatura* deal.

But I digress.

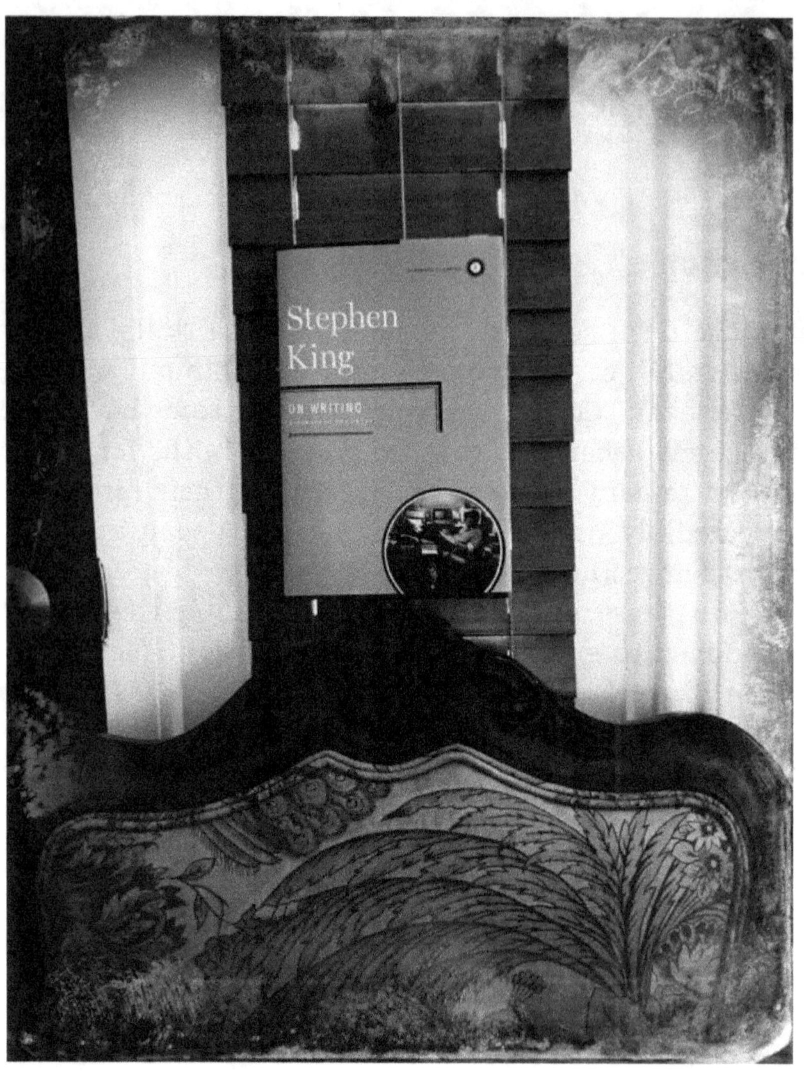

Honor has not to be won; it must only not be lost.
- Arthur Schopenhauer

Another (Fellow) Writer Who
Writes For The Buzz

He Verily Speaks My Language, Woohoo!

Let me put it this way: this guy speaks my language, woohoo! Look, I'm a stickler for details: If anything brings about my downfall—other than, of course, my penchant for digressing—it will be my fanatical devotion to details. With that, I now share with you the very first time that I came upon the word "row"... Not the pedestrian, "row" as in "row, row, row your boat" but as in the seldom-used variant, "a noisy quarrel or dispute (Pronounced so as to rhyme with, um, "cow"). Cowabunga. And cows galore for sure.

The Loss Of Innocence

So this is my loss of innocence as far as the word "row" is concerned—in Chapter XI of a slim book that was assigned reading in high school—as I encountered it in these opening words from Chapter XI of the Hilton book. And mind you, not the hotel, the book, heh:

> *AND THEN THE ROW with Ralston. Funny thing, Chips had never liked him; he was efficient, ruthless, ambitious, but not, somehow, very likable. He had, admittedly, raised the status of Brookfield as a school, and for the first time in memory there was a longish waiting list. Ralston was a live wire; a fine power transmitter, but you had to beware of him.*
> *- James Hilton (Goodbye, Mr. Chips: A Novel)*

I will add only this much: This was made all the more interesting—as if there were a shortage of interesting things on my grubby hand in those days—by the fact that one of my classmates was named Rao! (Rhymes with the word "Dow" from the finance world, and *not* with the word "DAO" from the software

world, at least not the pronunciation variant I'm familiar with which, by the way, rhymes with "mayo"). I leave it to *your* imagination—after all, as a reader, you've got to do *some* work—to conjure up some irreverent word-playing fun we high schoolers had around that time in our lives. Ah, when we all felt invincible, with scarcely a worry on our mind other than what we would have for lunch, when we were young and free, when...
Um, I *do* digress at times, *don't* I? (Hint: You're supposed to reply with an emphatic *No* here)

Robitussin! We Say No.

Okay, what you got above was a taste of the fruits from my fanatical devotion to details. How about a dose of an innocuous digression such as the one coming up next? Ready? And please—*puh-leeze*—do please tell me that my essays don't taste like *Robitussin.*
So my encounter—think *Close Encounters of the Third Kind*—with that malfeasant scumbag of a word ("row") was from *Goodbye, Mr. Chips: A Novel.* Yep, since it was assigned reading in high school, it obviously tasted like medicine *at* that time.

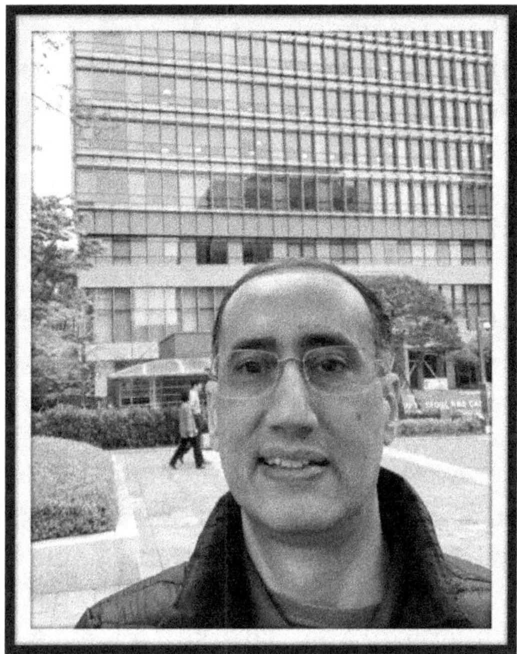

Enough. We're Not Taking Any More Medicine

Enough talk of cough medicine. Let's bring some medicine-free joy back with some impenitent verses of rhyme, shall we? Here we go!

Watch the writer precariously perched atop a turret, hope-lessly in love with words,
See the improbable poet, poised on a tuffet, eating his own words and curds

Watch as a software craftsman revels in the trenches where code is made in the shade,
See him pushing back derelict fronds and fern glades with the gentle nudge of a blade

Watch as his implacable foe—the bard—bends to erect a

laughable house of cards,
He, meanwhile—jujitsu-style—blithely tend to his dis-
tributed computing shards.
- Akram Ahmad ("Pushing the Envelope"—yet another
random poem by a writer, blogger, software craftsman,
son, husband, father, brother, and friend)

Since we are on the subject of schooldays, I might as well mention that—and this is going *way* down memory lane—I attended Aitchison College (a high school, really, but the word "college" somehow stuck, so there you have it). Aitchison is modeled after Eton and Harrow in England. We did some pretty cool stuff there while I was a student; in brief, taking part in any and all essay-writing competitions that I could barge my way into is one memory that pops into my head. But I digress.

Oh, one other memory that I'd like to wedge in—especially since we were talking about Eton and Harrow above—is that of a brilliant essay written by a fellow Aitchisonian (a classmate in fact, who went on to attend the University of Cambridge) that was entitled *Why Aitchison?* That essay explored, among other things, the theme of how

The battle of Waterloo was won on the playing fields of Eton

Uh-Oh, Here Comes The Stickler-For-Details

Once again, being the stickler for details that I am, I did some investigation and found that the quotation above is actually a misquote. It's no big deal; the correct quotation is the following one:

> *Probably the battle of Waterloo was won on the playing-*
> *fields of Eton, but the opening battles of all subsequent*
> *wars have been lost there.*

Allow me just one more digression: won't you please indulge

me? Look up the first year (of an education) at Harrow—pretty cool stuff—as made memorable by Winston Churchill.

Having said all that about Harrow and Churchill, I must hasten to emphasize—lest anyone jump to the *totally* wrong conclusion that I'm some prissy aristocrat—that I *have* always, and *will* always, strongly identify with the proletariat. I say so unabashedly, and not with a little vehemence; I wouldn't have it any other way. Oh no!

With that, let's bring it the Mr. Cool of writing, the king who shall pontificate on the craft of writing awesomeness: Stephen King.

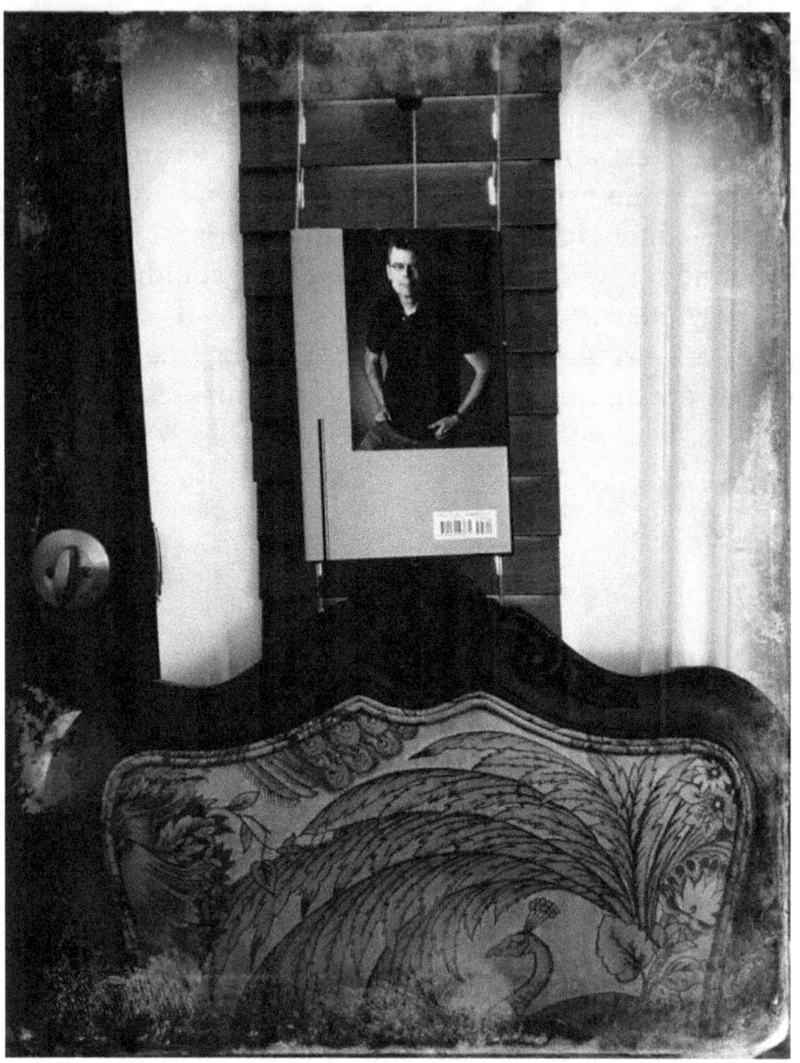

I tell you: When it comes to the craft of writing and stuff, it's in King that I've found a kindred soul of a fellow proletariat.

Then There Was A Search
(One Fueled by Magic)

I want it to be known that there *are* individuals in my life whom I revere; when they read this, they'll know who I have in mind as I write this. There *are,* also, individuals in my life who keep me turned on to the joy of crafting prose; they bring the feeling, they bring the fire and I know that they, too, will know who I have in mind as I write this.

 What do we have here, perched atop a random bookshelf in my home?

Aha, my copy of *Practical Probabilistic Programming* (Manning Publications) by Avi Pfeffer...

What gives? Why is it propped up at the top? Why?

Read on to find out!

Parting Thoughts

What Did Make It Into This Essay...

There was *so* much more I had wished to add, but... Yep, time and space constraints raise their heads—goodness, don't I know all about it, being the engineer and computer scientist that I am! Take heart: there will be another time, there will be another essay.

I promise I'll be back to tie in several loose threads next time; can't leave you all hanging like that, now can I?

...And What Couldn't Make It

Exploring the connection—concord as well as dissonance, at least as I see it—between the themes each in King's advice on writing and McPhee's advice on the same

More—*much* more, I promise you—on that tantalizing *sprezzatura* accolade from well-wishers; once again, it's *not* a carbonated drink, okay? Um, I *think* not. Lemme double-check, though, for good measure

I need to commune with code—not always but more often than not in the Scala and Java programming languages—so maybe I'll tie that in as well; how? I myself don't know at this point, but we'll figure it out together. Remember what I once said about how I cannot *not* write (prose)? Ditto for writing (computer code). So there, dear Reader.

A unique dialog—in the style of *The Matrix* trilogy—in which The Oracle and your blogger will be engaged face-to-face. It will be rather intense (just a fair warning for the faint of heart; that's not *you*, though, right?)

A dive, or two, into Saroo Brierley's captivating book entitled *A Long Way Home: A Memoir...* I've only begun reading it but it's looking terrific already!

Some new thoughts on the practice of Reactive Programming— <u>built atop my *existing* understanding</u>—as inspired by my mentor Jonas Boner; my assessment so far of the terrain, should you wish to look it up, can meanwhile be found by way of my recommendation for Jonas.

A Time To Give Thanks...

As Americans, we recently celebrated Thanksgiving. It's the traditional time of the year for families to come together yet again, partaking of each other's company—hey, let's not forget the delicious food either—thereby reaffirming the ties that bind. Importantly, Thanksgiving is *also* a time to reach out to neighbors and strengthen the bonds of kinship: the picture below (which I selected from the public domain and subsequently transformed to daguerreotype) of pilgrims in New England reaching to their American Indian neighbors perfectly illustrates this point.

Last, but certainly not the least, we will—again, this, too, in a future essay—also chat some about a remarkable book called *Practical Probabilistic Programming* (Manning Publications) by Avi Pfeffer, with a Foreword by Stuart Russell (co-author, with Peter Norvig, of my all-time favorite text on Artificial Intelligence). It has some of the slickest code in the Scala programming language that I have set my eyes on; *much* more to follow, in fact, on *Practical Probabilistic Programming* so stay tuned.

LETTER VI: STELLAR SENTENCES GET GANGSTA TREATMENT

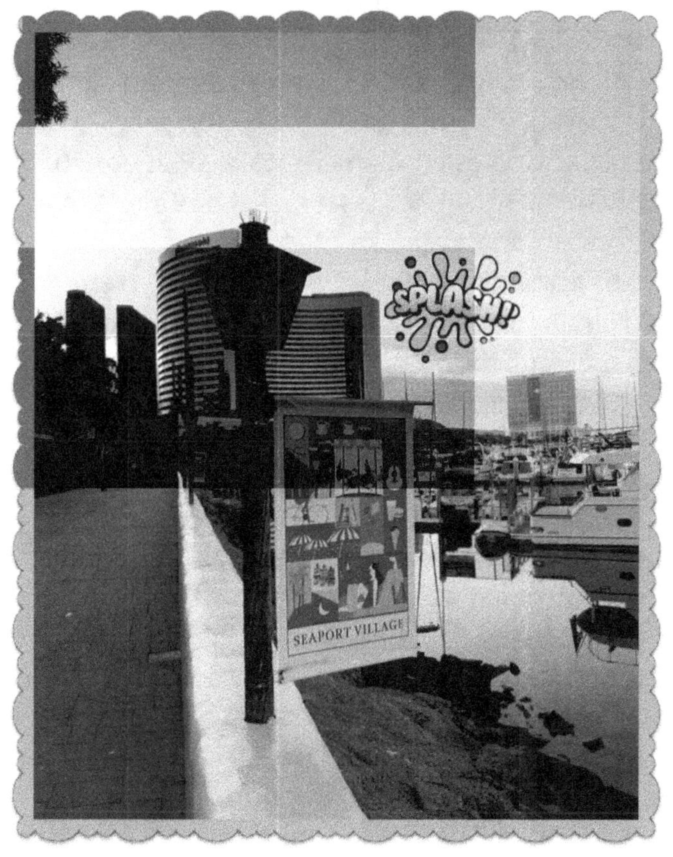

Explaining Metaphysics to the nation—
I wish he would explain his Explanation
- Lord Byron (from Don Juan: Dedication)

Dear Reader,

I'm going to let you in on a secret. *Psst...* Don't tell any-one, but this whole metaphysics business—for example the hilarious Lord Byron quote above—is nothing more than fancy words for eminently down-to-earth ideas. Let's just say that the phenomenal wordsmith Byron, in his tongue-in-cheek remark above, was merely stating the obvious. So yeah.

And taking that line of thought to its logical conclusion is the business of the letter—the sixth one, I believe—that you hold in your hand. Chameleon-like, we're going to take some stellar sentences and change their coloration, extreme makeover-style, making sure to have some transformational fun along the way; think metamorphosis, *Kafkaesque* or otherwise.

But first a quick word.

Writing: Sheer, Unalloyed Joy

It goes like this: Writing was never, *ever* meant to be boring; if anyone tells you otherwise, dispatch them my way so I can have a word with them.

Writing is, first and foremost, all about having fun with words and sentences and such. I scratched my head for a while and came to the conclusion that I could scarcely do better than illustrate the sentiment—that all about having fun—by an extended and admittedly jocular take on some of the greatest writers of all time.

Sparing Your Sensibilities

Brutha'—and sista'—we're gonna' be revisiting some of the loveliest writing known to mankind—and womankind to be sure —but with a twist: We'll do all that from the vantage point of *gangsta* speak. (Even as I invite you to cross over the threshold of this seemingly innocent letter, my feelings, they be tinged with sympathy for you; should I *really* be doing this to you, dear Reader?)

Such was the gravity of the question with which your blogger grappled during the past 24 hours. I'm tellin' ya, the life of a writer ain't easy; it sure ain't a bowl of cherries.

Whoa, methinks I be getting ahead of myself so I be holdin' my horses now!

Ah yes, so there will be gangsta speak in just a bit—mounds and *mounds* of it, I promise—but first I need to spare your sensibilities by indoctrinating you *ever*-so-slowly into gangsta speak itself, into the hood', as I like to call it, you and others, playa' by playa'. (See, didn't I tell you a moment ago that my feelings, they be tinged raw with sympathy for ya, debating as I did to the last moment whether I even *ought* to be doing this to you.)

The Decision Is To Proceed
Full Steam Ahead

For an essay with a title like that—"*Stellar Sentences Get Gangsta Treatment*"—I got to thinking, "*Hmm... Where do I even begin?*"

Yo, here's the lowdown: Whether it's the starving, starry-eyed boy in the candy shop, or the enervated mosquito that has randomly buzzed its way into an oversubscribed nudist colony, or say the inveterate book-lover as she takes the step in crossing the threshold of Harvard's gargantuan Widener Memorial Library, the question remains the same, "Where do I *begin?*"

Let's face it: Sentences are, after all, what make prose sing and poetry weep; they also happen to be the irreducible elements wherefrom we bootstrap our thinking; and they are, too, after all, the indestructible building blocks—imagine a horde of tingling, *LEGO*-like widgets all-abuzz—with which we assemble and thereafter scaffold the edifice of our writing.

The Elements (aka Journey Pit-stops) In Our Collage

This time, and just for you—though this be defenestration by another name—I'm going to let the cat out of the bag from the get go. So here we go.

The Cast

Yes, even before I regale you in the wherewithal of how I came to make these choices—my selection of the finest sentences to receive gangsta treaement—I want you to know the names of the stellar writers who wrote them (Some of these names will be instantly recognizable, others perhaps less so). Here, then, are the authors who have either (1) already entered the Pantheon of writing greatness, or (2) are well on their way to crossing its threshold:

1. William Shakespeare
2. Charles Dickens
3. Samuel Johnson
4. Robert Frost
5. T.S. Eliot
6. Kitty Fassett
7. Emily Dickinson

While there is *some* significance to the order in which the names appear on the list above—for example I wedge everyone between the two supremely gifted writers that Shakespeare and

Dickinson are universally acknowledged as being—the names appear pretty much in the order in which some especially memorable sentences of the respective writers' percolated up through the nooks and crannies of my mind, and into my consciousness.

One More Time, With Emotion

Here, then, I present those seven writers again, this time with a title of the accompanying commentary—and all that stash coming up quick, fellow gangstas—on their craft, *gangsta*-style of course:

1. **William Shakespeare**
   —Finessing The Duality Of Comparing And Contrasting
2. **Charles Dickens**
   —Scaffolding With The Power Of Balance And Proportion
3. **Samuel Johnson**
   —Injecting Ethereal Layers Of Similarity And Difference
4. **Robert Frost**
   —Directing Emotions With Deftness
5. **T.S. Eliot**
   —Corralling Fleeting Remembrances With Strokes Of Genius
6. **Kitty Fassett**
   —Harnessing The Desiderata By Discarding Inessentials
7. **Emily Dickinson**
   —Carving Astonishing Feats Of Imagination

And hey, before anyone impugns my motives, gets all roiled up, and suggests that yours truly should be placed in a remedial arithmetic class—I know, I *know,* I've dragged in seven authors despite brashly claiming that I'd be treating you to the nebulously-worded moniker *"Stellar Sentences Get Gangsta Treat-*

ment"—let me say in my defense, by way of a rhetorical question, *"Hast thou heard of thine Baker's dozen?"*

There's something magical about the number seven, amirite?

(The actual story is a bit more complicated, and you don't want me digressing no moh', or *do* you? *Easy* there now. I was *just* checking... Sheesh, some folks *do* get all roiled up over piddling stuff.)

Check The Route...

So here we are, on the threshold of diving into the sheer loveliness of some sparkling sentences. And even as you reflect on the sublime architecture of the Sydney Opera House reflected in the waters on its embankment, I invite you to spend a few moments pondering over the following question:

Does art follow life or does life follow art?

With that, we now be diving into the uncharted waters of gangsta land; here be dragons, amirite?

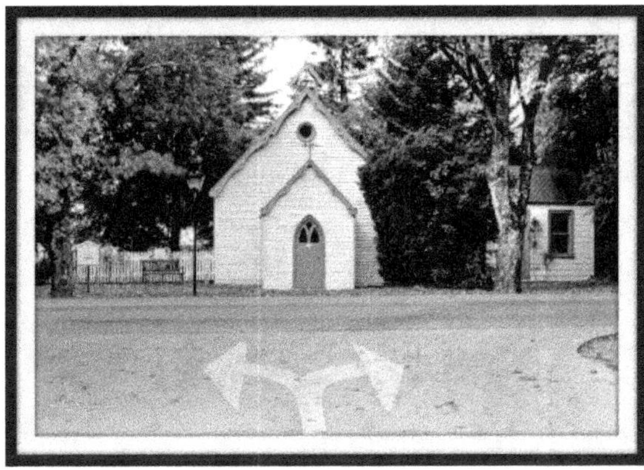

*1. William Shakespeare (Finessing
The Duality Of Comparing
And Contrasting)*

The Original (William Shakespeare)

*As Caesar loved me, I weep for him; as he was fortunate,
I rejoice at it; as he was valiant, I honour him: but, as he
was ambitious, I slew him. There is tears for his love; joy
for his fortune; honour for his valour; and death for his
ambition.*
- William Shakespeare (in The Tragedy Of Julius Caesar)

The Gangsta Remix:

Brutha', you gotta somehow keep love in the hood. Your man
Brutus knew, however, that *too* much love make you soft and
dat ain't happenin' around here; gotta keep the hood good, so
chill, *RIP* (and I ain't talkin' *Rip* van Winkle, yo.) So Brutus did
the hood a solid and straight merc'd Caesar with a dagger; yo,
that's when we got Caesar all choking up and saying things like,
"*You Too, Brutus*" (in the Roman language of course!). But da bot-

tom line still be: *another* one bites the dust, and that why we got Brutus 'splainin above 'bout why he be killing Julius Caesar, amirite?

2. Charles Dickens (Scaffolding With The Power Of Balance And Proportion)

The Original (Charles Dickens)

Fog everywhere. Fog up the river, where it flows among green aits and meadows; fog down the river, where it rolls defiled among the tiers of shipping and the water-side pollutions of a great (and dirty) city. Fog on the Essex marshes, fog on the Kentish heights. Fog creeping into the cabooses of collier-brigs; fog lying out on the yards, and hovering in the rigging of great ships; fog drooping on the gunwales of barges and small boats. Fog in the eyes and throats of ancient Greenwich pensioners, wheezing by the firesides of their wards; fog in the stem and bowl of the afternoon pipe of the wrathful skipper, down in his close cabin; fog cruelly pinching the toes and fingers of his shivering little 'prentice boy on deck. Chance people on the bridges peeping over the parapets into a nether sky of fog, with fog all round them, as if they were up in a balloon, and hanging in the misty clouds.
- Charles Dickens (in his novel Bleak House)

The Gangsta Remix:

Darn, I'm tellin' ya, that Dickens fella' one mean writer; he be painting pictures with his words; and he got the art of writing down smack like no one else. A cool-headed homie, he nonetheless be writing from the wellspring of his fertile imagination, settin' the readin' and writin' world on fire. Remember the lovely song *Nightshift* (by *The Commodores*) where they be singin' all 'bout soul/R&B singer Jackie (Wilson) and rememberin' us dis' by the *Commodores*, from their song, *Nightshift*: "*Jackie (Jackie), hey whatchyou doing now?*"

No doubt about it, Dickens be one mean writer and prolific, too—settin' the readin' and writin' world on fire—but he always be serious, talkin' grim business that make you scratch your head. My grade school-teacha', though, he tell me hisself, many moons ago, that I be doing myself a favor by reading Dickens; he sez to me, "*It be good for you, it gonna broaden your horizons, and make your mind groove in the right directions*," or something close to that is what I remember him telling me, my oh-so kind grade school-teacha' *hisself*.)

While Dickens—now *he* sure was one dickens of a writer—got the power of balance and the power of proportion, it's in their *mixin'* that the mean brutha' outdo everyone. Erryone and their brother you care to mention, yo, he outdone them all. So even though he sometimes be writing all prissy about fog and other touchy-feely stuff, he make you think; he wrap you up in all kinda' exquisite atmospheres with, as I was alluding to earlier, his smashing-good word-painting. He be my mayne man, my homie; he the real thang'.

3. Samuel Johnson (Injecting Ethereal Layers Of Similarity And Difference)

The Original (Samuel Johnson)

The style of Dryden is capricious and varied; that of Pope is cautious and uniform. Dryden observes the motions of his own mind; Pope constrains his mind to his own

roles of composition. Dryden is sometimes vehement and rapid; Pope is always smooth, uniform, and gentle. Dryden's page is a natural field, rising into inequalities, and diversified by the varied exuberance of abundant vegetation; Pope's is a velvet lawn, shaven by the scythe, and levelled by the roller."
- Samuel Johnson (in The Works of Samuel Johnson)

The Gangsta Remix:

Check it—the two rams in the picture above ain't no Alexander Pope and no John Dryden. They both good homies, always dressing up real decent, wearing ironed shirts and shirt-ties, their hair all combed-back slick like *Johhny Depp*, with gobs of da real thang, that *LA Looks* hair-stylin' gel; Pope and Dryden weren't all that bad either... Hey, just checkin', just checkin', cuz' no rams wearing no *LA Looks*. Just wanna' make sure you all stay awake. No napping around heah'. (Disclaimer: I ain't—never was and never will—hustling no hair-styling products.)

Ennyhow, here's what went down with Samuel Johnson (SJ) ramlin—err, *rambling*—about Pope and Dryden, the dynamic duo: As SJ be tellin' us, Pope real uptight, always makin' sure he cover his rear; he don't want nobody put the smack on him for violating uniformity in his writing. Dryden, on the other hand, he one cool goose, always chillin' and going with da flow (he be my style of writer!)

While Pope give his reader prissy velvet lawns, Dryden be groovin, giving us readers the real deal, giving us the scoop at Ground Zero: Dryden never talking down to us homies. He level with us, and he *level* us—in a good way—with dis mighty machine the steamroller, amirite?

4. Robert Frost (Directing Emotions With Deftness)

The Original (Robert Frost)

No tears in the writer, no tears in the reader. No surprise for the writer, no surprise for the reader. For me the initial delight is in the surprise of remembering something I didn't know I knew. I am in a place, in a situation, as if I had materialized form cloud or risen out of the ground. There is a glad recognition of the long lost and the rest follows. Step-by-step the wonder of unexpected supply keeps growing. The impressions most useful to my purpose seem always those I was unaware of and so made no note of at the time when taken, and the conclusion is come to that like giants we are always hurling experience ahead of us to pave the future with against the day and when we

may Want to strike a line of purpose across it for some-where. We enjoy the straight crookedness of a good walk-ing stick. Modern instruments of precision are being used to make things crooked as if by eye and hand in the old days. I tell how there may be a better wildness of logic than of inconsequence. But the logic is backward, in retrospect, after the act. It must be more felt than seen ahead like prophecy.
- Robert Frost (in The Figure a Poem Makes)

The Gangsta Remix:

Frosty be one of them three solitary poets to make my list, as-suming we're not counting Billy Shakes as a full-fledged poet—his sonnets of course are a phenomenon to behold in their own right though he shaking the world of prose real good—and de-serves high marks for slinging some amazing verses. Actually, what you got above is an example of Frosty's prose, though he still be talking smack about his real love: verses of poetry.

This gangsta' be a master of the turn of phrase. Check this: "*No tears in the writer, no tears in the reader. No surprise for the writer, no surprise for the reader...*". This ain't no fool we are dealing with; he's our own homie, so chill (If only he had done less of that Apple picking—I don't like no apples cuz' I'm strictly a coffee kinda' guy and not dig da jejune you know, bro'—and more of Starbucks' Coffee, I be talkin' even *more* highly of Frosty now.)

5. T.S. Eliot (Corralling Fleeting Re-membrances With Strokes Of Genius)

The Original (T.s. Eliot)

*The yellow fog that rubs its back upon the window panes,
The yellow smoke that rubs its muzzle on the window panes*

Licks its tongue into the corners of the evening,
Lingers on the pools that stand in drains, Lets fall upon its
back the soot that falls from chimneys,
Slips by the terrace, makes a sudden leap,
And seeing that it's a soft October night,
Curls once about the house, and falls asleep
- T.S. Eliot (from his poem The Love Song of J. Alfred Pru-
frock)

The Gangsta Remix:

Check the curled-up cat that be all asleep in the pic atop this element in our collage... She be a good cat. Much the same, poetry be all good, my sayz unabashedly. It's for all reg' homies like you and me. Brutha', poetry be the distillation of reams of prose; how cool is that.

We now be entering the realm of corralling fleeting remembrances with strokes of genius (Different stroke for different folks, amirite?) And who betta' to round up them evanescent thoughts than T.S. Eliot, a homie way smarta' than all da otha' ganstas' who be writing poetry with valor.

Brutha', anyone even remember what I wrote up 'bout another poetry-slinging thug by the name of W.H. Auden in a recent essay? (Hint: Say *"Yes!"* And keep your blogger's heart from breakin' yo, so I know you be paying attention to what I be writing, or I be preachin' to the choir sound asleep?)

You know something? T.S. Eliot owes a boatload of intellectual debt to Billy Shakes. So our mayne man—who else but Billy Shakes, the leader of the pack who put down the smack on the readin' and writin' world—the fella' who be leading our list of writing loveliness, is still the biggest dawg of 'em all.

Even though he sling lovely verses of poetry, it's the world of *prose* that he be shaking and turnin' upside down! And so I be sharing a ditty I wrote up to honor my nemesis, the Bard:

While Auden may be the modern new thang whose poetry be pelting you both soft and hard,
Yo, it's still the inimitable Bard who be rollin' with the punches and holdin' every single card
And so it is that I hold aloft the message I myself wrote up on this tri-fold placard
"Yo, words never had it so good as when they were in the safe hands of the Bard."

6. Kitty Fassett (Harnessing The Desiderata By Discarding Inessentials)

The Original (Kitty Fassett)

He had a mischievous streak and I remember his instructions to an employee on the makings of a martini: "Fill a large glass with ice, pour in a jigger of gin and just a drop of vermouth," he said. "Then when my wife isn't

looking add two more jiggers of gin." He was an incorrigible punster, too, but most of all a gifted poet. One day he started quoting the first lines of his fiftieth reunion poem: "Return to jubilation! Scorn the woe – of mortal age and time's relentless flow! — Do you know who wrote that?" "You did, Pop," I replied. He was disappointed. He'd hoped I would guess Milton. It was a good poem, although I resented one of its stanzas that stated that astronauts had returned to earth "on wings of mathematics." When it came to mathematics he just couldn't let go. I liked his limericks better.
- Kitty Fassett (from her essay Pop's War: My Father, the CIA, and the Green Death)

The Gangsta Remix:

This sista' got mojo like nobody else. While Kitty Fassett may not be a household name, yet, cuz' she be an unassuming writer, she be second to none, writing with peerless clarity, grace, wit, and verve (Sista' got the creds too: degree from Vassar, she went on to be one of the most refined pianist evah').

So I be havin' the distinct honor of featuring a marvelous essay she had wrote up—my readers who come to this blog on the reg will clearly remember how this sista' saved you all from my quotidian prose, once anyway for crying out loud—and not too long ago either. That's right, this playa' be drooling over what she write, it so good: I decided to set my sights high, and be tellin' myself, morning and evening now for a long time (and especially when on my knees, right before going to bed, with my grubby hands outstretched, imploring the heavens in prayer), that one day I be writing like this sista'.

Here's what went down: Me, I be literal in my writing—and elsewhere as those in the know be knowin'—putting the whole thang on the page; she, on the other hand, be showing us

through her writing how to go about harnessing them desiderata by discarding inessentials.

To take just one example—straight out of the excerpt above
—she be discarding all kinda' inessentials in the last two sentences ("*When it came to mathematics he just couldn't let go. I
liked his limericks better.*") and distilling reams and reams of related thoughts into that above-mentioned lean and mean pair
of gangsta' sentences, amirite?

(Hey, were it left to me, heavens-forbid, had I instead gone
about capturing them same thoughts—you guessed it right for a
change—I would've blithely plastered reams and reams of paper
with pools and pools of ink. But not her; she be supremely
gifted. Sista' got a way with words.

Check this. What I got here is serious laughing gas—by who else
but Gass who be projecting breathtakin' acts of balance—which
will illustrate what I got in mind when I said that, "*Sista' got a
way with words.*" (And you may look up the glorious details in
the Dedication section in another essay).

Sista' be doin' the writing hood such a solid—making us all
proud in the process—that from now on I be calling her Little
Red Writin' Hood. But there's a catch…

Right, only prollem is, she so refined—dad-gum, didn't I tell you
a short while ago that sista' be one of the most refined pian-
ists evah'?—that she prolly don't want no bizness with us gangstas… If she somehow find out, heaven-forbid, that I be writing
like thiiiis, she put the smack on me, and I be out of the writing
bizness.

Forever…

You prolly be thanking yo' lucky stars when that happen, sayin'
stuff like "good riddance to bad rubbish", but I be a forlorn writing homie, all tattered and torn, amirite?

*7. Emily Dickinson (Carving
Astonishing Feats Of Imagination)*

The Original (Emily Dickinson)

The soul selects her own society,
Then shuts the door;
On her divine majority
Obtrude no more.

Unmoved, she notes the chariot's pausing
At her low gate;
Unmoved, an emperor is kneeling
Upon her mat.

I've known her from an ample nation

Choose one;
Then close the valves of her attention
Like stone
- Emily Dickinson

The Gangsta Remix:

Dat soul check her own biddy,
Then she slam the door shut;
On her righteousness
Mess up no moh'.

Summodat distraction cruisin' by
At her shack;
Trippin' on the knee
On the rug.

My choice be from mighty big country
Choosin' uno;
Then shut out other homies,
Who went down like the rock.

Parting Thoughts

I'm gonna' level with you now... (By the way, regarding the poem above, was that writing greatness or *was* that writing greatness?)
Anyhow, here's the thang: My verses are obviously ground zero, both literally and metaphorically. Yo, now why did I say that? Here's why: I used that million-dollar word ("metaphorically") cuz' of the symbolism of the epicenter of a phenomenon and I used another of them million-dollar words ("literally") cuz' of what I've shared above with you all in my hood—Emily's rocking' poem above as an example of her at the top of her phenomenal writin' game—is writing greatness, amirite?

I'm tellin' ya, Emily is da one who mercs poetry, never ceasing to amaze her fans (yours truly notably among them!) as her sentences float around like butterflies—in the selfsame unbearable lightness of being—lifting the glory of verse to dizzying heights. Darn, others then came long and getta free ride, or so they thin... But you know what? There still ain't no one—many tried their hand in futility at emulating her—who be writin' poetry not half as good as hers (Thang is, her impersonators try to do what she did, and then when it ain't working out, they all bent outta shape, amirite?)

Baddest (I Mean, The Best.)

She bad, the baddest of all the poets who ever lived. Sista' betta' than all them Yeatses, Keatses, Plaths (all put *together*, brutha'). You name em', and my sista' Emily outdone em' all (Frosty approach her virtuosity a bit, and at times only, but then he get all bogged down in the mire of roads-not-taken and boondoggles like that. What else can I say?)
Emily be the baddest, which is why she get to have the last word in the hood, our Pantheon hood of writing greatness!

Collage Be Done

The collage be done now, but I gotta slip this in edgewise: See them two pedestrians strolling in the pic above? Brutha', that be Emily, along with some homie whose name be lost to history. She be lightin' the way for future generations of writers—those crafting verses of poetry as well as those crafting lines of prose—in a way no sista' (or brutha' for that matter) ever done before...

We Done Now (For Real)?

Emily, the tremendous writing inspiration that your writings are, to you—and reaching back here through the incorporeal mists of time—I pose the following rhetorical question with utmost sincerity: Why don't we, the readers and writers of the world, *stay* just a little bit longer? Can't we *play*, just a little bit longer?

◆ ◆ ◆

LETTER VII: YER EDINBURGH ODE TO MICROSERVICES

The machine does not isolate man from the great prob-
lems of nature but plunges him more deeply into them.
- Antoine de Saint-Exupery

Dear Reader,

In this penultimate letter, if you're still with me—hey come back!—I continue to let you in on the *second* (and somewhat ancillary, though no less important) part of the secret that I had broached in the *prior* letter: Writing is meant to be a fun activity.

(Ah, the fact that you haven't dispatched anyone my way anyone who would misguidedly have you believe, heaven forbid, that writing was meant to be boring, bodes well.)

Odes Less Traveled

Here, then, is that *second,* ancillary aspect of the joy of writing: Poetry may be the ode—I mean, the road—less traveled, but it sure isn't a barred one. So go forth and sling a verse or two: You may be a poet, and just didn't know it. Heh.

With that, we come to the heart of the matter, of this letter: You see, I tried my hands at it (i.e. poetry) *yet* again and have lived to tell you that tale.

The Tale.

Attending the Open IoT Europe Summit (in Edinburgh, Scotland) was an amazing experience. I returned from Europe just a couple of days ago. Yep, Edinburgh is an amazing city, filled with kind-hearted people: That made the Open IoT Summit *extra* special on top of the technical agenda that was packed with exciting presentations, working sessions, and discussions!

The EdgeX Foundry open-source project—it's hosted by The Linux Foundation—is going places, so it's especially gratifying that a substantial chunk of my waking hours go (as a committer on EdgeX) into the fun work of helping change the world of IoT as we know it today.

Ebullient, Enticing Edinburgh

Well, whether it was the IoT *Summit* or the alluring Edinburgh *surroundings*—likely a *combination* of the two—that did it, I was inspired to write up some light verses one evening in Edinburgh when I had an idle hour or two to pass in the comfort of my pleasant hotel room. Today, I added a handful more verses—yo, someone stop Akram from writing even more while you still can, someone, *please*—and which I unabashedly offer here.

Picture This

And what good would be a blog post that did not have at least an accompanying picture or two?

I jest not, so all you bonnie lassies and laddies, find yer pictures right after the verses that now follow, because this yin*—when you are ready, go to the end for a translation of this and a handful of similar, inimitably Scottish words and phrases—is as good as it gets around here in our (Programming Digressions) digs.

Yer Edinburgh Ode to Microservices

They ask, in all seriousness, this innocent question,
"Will my microservices forever remain performant?"
They might as well, instead, ask this question,
"Will production problems evermore remain dormant?"

*But first—and curiously for some—we now unabashedly
switch to (non-alternating) pairs of verses,
So there, 'cuz the first four lines atop have already war-
ranted much juggles and rehearses!*

*Oh, laddie, so you say that some of yer microservices are
on fire,
Yo, you should have alerted me right away for something
so dire!*

*But have no fear, to the rescue will come tracing,
And handily solve the problem yer facing*

*Do tell me—please do—that you've already instrumented
yer source code,
If not, all is still not lost, no laddie it isn't, and yes, that's
me doon the road*

*Anyway, hey, hey, hey now! I ain't calling anyone an eejit
or that they be straying into the land of weed,
Aye, I hear you, lassie: Other, higher-priority matters had
beckoned, meanwhile, and "you're a long time deid"*

*All I be saying is that when it comes to monitoring sys-
tems with many a wee—and occasionally waylaid—moving part,
It would be best if all components communicate in the
same, simple ways, lest hopes of tracing them do depart!*

*Let's divine what ails your darling system on which you
have plainly showered much care,
Though, as I understand it, for its upkeep and instrumen-
tation you did not quite prepare*

*All is not lost because—with your lovely workflows in
place—you can still do stuff to monitor and estimate,*

Aye, mate, surely, to take a message-oriented perspective,
you need to monitor yer message-flow rate

There's nothing quite like getting eyeballs to peer into the
workings of your application,
That is, should you wish to avoid sleepless nights and
many a similar complication

You see, we expect great things from the exciting micro-
services revolution,
They are, after all, the next step in the remarkable SOA
evolution

Microservices, to be sure, have emerged from the molten-
pit kindled by flames of a brave new world,
Arrr, domain-driven design, continuous delivery, and
systems at scale, to use but a few bonnie word

The clamor for scaling, resilience, ease-of-deployment,
and composability verily could not be left unaddressed,
And was answered—in the shape of wee bonnie microser-
vices of course!—by a legion of developers, all self-pos-
sessed

Aye, but there be no silver bullet, lassie, so mark those
words as you merrily go down that road,
Noo go on, don't you be looking at me with them forlornly
moist eyes: yes, this was the ode!

Translation Of Scottish Words And Phrases

1. ***Yin:*** One
2. ***Eejit:*** Idiot
3. ***Deid*** [as in "*You're a long time **deid**"*]: The English translation of

this one—and I *love* it so—is "*You're a long time dead*", and if you're thinking that's a pretty obvious statement but are still not sure what it means, try this... (As in, take the blue pill or the red!) "*Enjoy life, because once you're dead you're going to be that way for a long time.*" Not *exactly* uplifting, but true all the same, eh?

4. **SOA:** Okay, okay, I get it. This buzzword (i.e. SOA) is not *quite* Scottish. But these three letters *do* serve as an acronym for the venerable **S**ervice **O**riented **A**rchitecture, the precursor, of course—remember, we should ever-so-often revisit the basics —to microservices. *Just* sayin'.

Great minds discuss ideas, average minds discuss events, small minds discuss people.
- Eleanor Roosevelt

O wonder!
How many goodly creatures are there here!
How beauteous mankind is! O brave new world
That has such people in it!
- William Shakespeare (in The Tempest)

There are no rules of architecture for a castle in the clouds.
- Gilbert K. Chesterton

There is only one thing in the world worse than being talked about, and that is not being talked about.
- Oscar Wilde

LETTER VIII:
BEAUTIFUL CODE,
BEAUTIFUL PROSE

Is it possible that software is not like anything else, that it is meant to be discarded: that the whole point is to always see it as a soap bubble?
- Alan J. Perlis

D ear Reader,

All good things come to an end. And these letters are no exception. Please know that my heart has delighted in sharing thoughts—along with a boatload of advice, insight, and what-not—with you. I thank you for making this a memorable time. In this, then, my eighth and final letter to you, I want to impart a somewhat more-philosophical stance on all things writing. It comes on the heels of two admittedly jocular letters—got to have fun sometime, right?—and is meant to bring this series of letters to a graceful end. Gravitas, as they say, is all with the ending. Mabye in the ending is our *beginning*.

How Abstract Should We Get?

Let's find exactly that out—especially since we programmer types spend a *lot* of time on abstractions in our code—by starting with a simple premise: What do beautiful code and beautiful prose even *look* like? Even more fundamentally, are these qualities not so abstract—to the point of being ethereal—that even *contemplating* their pursuit would be akin to tilting at windmills? Clearly, there is no arbiter to pontificate and decide this matter. There *are*, though, some guiding principles that may fruitfully lead us down a cherry-lined avenue of discovery.

Rigor In Beauty

Recall that we humans have pursued beauty in many a realm. Consider, for example, what the British mathematician and philosopher Bertrand Russell had to say on this elemental, yet elusive, quality:

> *Mathematics, rightly viewed, possesses not only truth, but supreme beauty—a beauty cold and austere, like that of sculpture, without appeal to any part of our weaker nature, without the gorgeous trappings of painting or music, yet sublimely pure, and capable of a stern perfection such as only the greatest art can show.*

That Russell chap sure could sling a hard-hitting phrase or two, and with virtuosity, too.

Remembrance Of Things Past

To this I add the seemingly anachronistic case of an observation by top-notch writer and Lisp hacker Peter Seibel. I have written an essay elsewhere regarding how the overwhelming impression which his book *Practical Common Lisp* left on my mind was that it had been written by someone who cares as much about the art of programming as he does for the craft of writing well.

An intriguingly glorious self-admission by Seibel in that book's *About the Author* section—that he is "either a writer-turned-programmer or a programmer-turned-writer"—underscores the seeming ambivalence.

And wow, does his command of both programming *and* writing shine throughout the book. Picking this thread—how one can care as much about their art as they do for the craft of writing well—leads me to briefly unroll the ball of yarn some more. Buckle up. (See the mobile ahoy, next to the Parcheesi board?) Here we go...

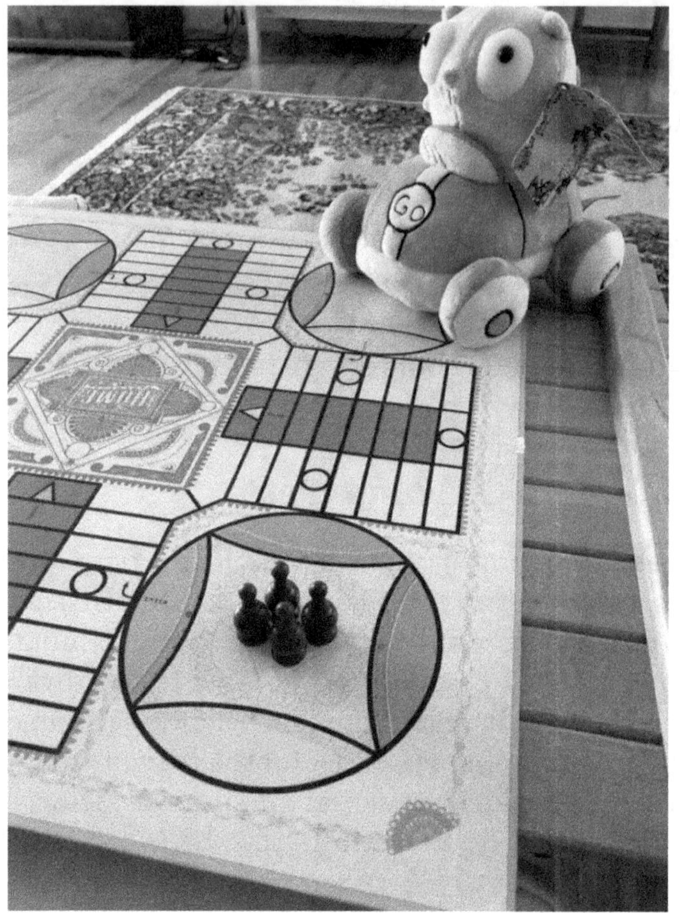

In literature, the ambition of the novice is to acquire the literary language; the struggle of the adept is to get rid of it.
- George Bernard Shaw

Of Rewriting (Or, Where Writing Really Happens)

My basic premise is that there exists a profound nexus between (software) code and prose: While the English language, or any other spoken language, for that matter, is clearly not Turing complete—I've heard, though, that COBOL occupied a fabled place somewhere between spoken and programming languages —the simple fact is that rewriting (spoken languages) maps directly to the programming notion of refactoring, which its originator, Martin Fowler, describes succinctly as

> *a disciplined technique for restructuring an existing body of code, altering its internal structure without changing its external behavior.*

To segue a bit, my late father, a chemical engineer by profession, and a man of uncommon decency and integrity, was a big fan of books by the prolific American author, the late James A. Michener, widely regarded for his meticulous research behind his books. So I can think of no better way to pay tribute to and honoring the memory of them both than by sharing this delightful quote by Michener, as cited by Professor John Trimble —more on *him* later—in Trimble's sage book on writing style entitled *Writing with Style: Conversations on the Art of Writing.* In reminding us of the sobering fact that writers "*...have accepted the grim reality that nine-tenths of all writing is rewriting...*", Trimble cites Michener as reflecting on his own work, sharing how he (Michener) never quite thought of himself as a good writer —now fancy that; oh, the humbleness—and instead envisioned himself as being up there with the world's greatest rewriters. And there you have it: humbleness and greatness, all rolled into one. (We are the richer for your sharing this gem with us, Professor Trimble.)

Back At The Ranch

Meanwhile, returning from the segue, and while still exploring the profound nexus between software code and prose, I'll add that software design patterns are a first-class attempt at reclaiming the beauty that may otherwise languish due to neglect and bit rot. This, too, has a direct counterpart in the crafting of prose; for more, I refer the interested reader to Professor John Trimble's *Writing with Style: Conversations on the Art of Writing.* (An. Awesome. Book.)

Another Magisterial Style Guide

Allow me to wedge in here, edgewise, the factoid that probably *the* preeminent tome on modern American usage—now in its fourth edition—is by yet another individual who cares as much about their art (the practice of law), as they do for the writing craft: Bryan Garner. His magisterial volume, simply entitled Garner's Modern American Usage (Oxford University Press), was received to wide acclaim, and for good reason; it simply happens to be one of those overwhelmingly rich yet can't-put-me-down volumes. A polymath of sorts, Garner has been recognized as a pioneer across a wide range of fields, including English usage, grammar, jurisprudence, legal advocacy, and is the president of the company—note here the marriage-made-in-heaven name—*LawProse Inc.*

Elsewhere in *Functional JavaScript,* Fogus reflects some more on beauty, pointing out how functions are a *"beautiful unit of work"*, allowing one to adhere to the long-practiced maxim in the UNIX community, set forth by Butler Lampson:

> *Make it run, make it right, make it fast.*

Likewise, *"functions-as-abstraction"* allow you to fulfill Kent Beck's similarly phrased mantra of test-driven development (TDD):

> *Make it run, then make it right, then make it fast*

Also in that book by Fogus (*Functional JavaScript*), and amplifying the same theme—how beauty and pragmatism are inextricably commingled—yet another noted software architect steps up the plate, and, going one step further, portrays the medium of software as being as malleable as putty. Good stuff.

An Eternal Golden Braid

Let's next turn our attention to the pursuit of beauty in the Pulitzer Prize-winning book Gödel, Escher, Bach: An Eternal Golden Braid whose author, Douglas Hofstadter, astonished the world with the publication of this mind-bending fugue of a book. This book's monumental impact was perhaps best heralded by the American popular mathematics and popular science writer Martin Gardner who elegantly summed it up by noting that

> *Every few decades an unknown author brings out a book of such depth, clarity, range, wit, beauty and originality that it is recognized at once as a major literary event. "Godel, Escher, Bach" is such a work.*

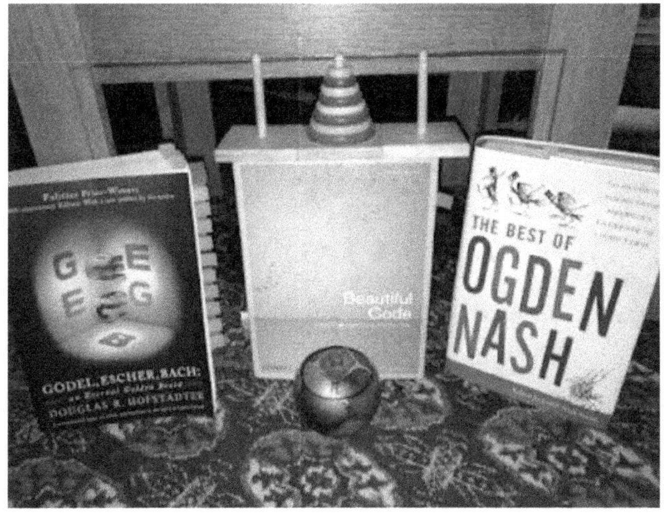

Finally, in laying to rest the thread we had picked up earlier—

how individuals can care as much about their chosen profession, presumably a non-writing one, as they do for the craft of writing well—let's check out an excerpt or two from the almost-sublime prose of an author whose name is likely alien to the majority of my fellow software designers, developers, and other technologists, though I may be pleasantly mistaken in my assumption: Allow me to introduce ace psychoanalyst Philip M. Bromberg, Ph.D.

It's simply impossible to even try to *contemplate* doing any sort of justice to the caliber of Bromberg's prose; the best antidote is for me to share a typical passage from this prolific writer. In particular—and I have a confession to make here—as someone who is smitten by the pixie-dust magic of em-dashes, I couldn't help but resonate with the impact wrought to great effect by Bromberg's use of em-dashes through the length and breadth of his seminal (written) works.

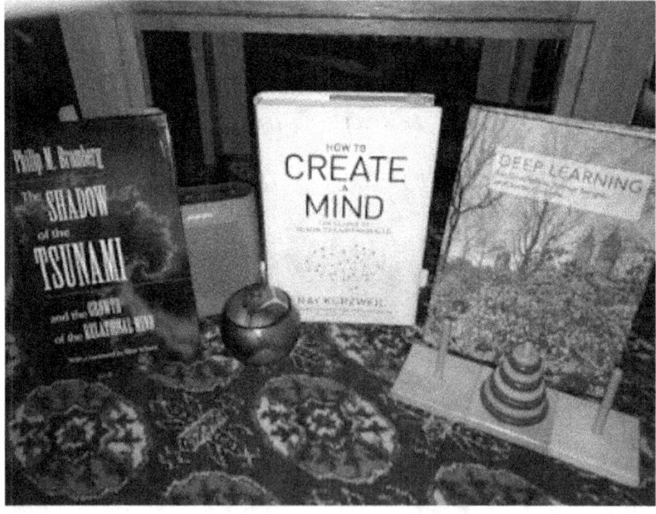

The Bard. The Man Himself.

Let's next turn to what English poet and playwright William Shakespeare, widely regarded as the greatest writer in the English language and the world's pre-eminent dramatist, had to say on beauty, by way of this monologue, spoken in the eponymous play by Prince Hamlet. And Shakespeare certainly had a way with words; here, he has angst-ridden Hamlet ruefully ponder over

> *What a piece of work is a man! How noble in reason! How infinite in faculties! In form and moving, how express and admirable! In action how like an angel!*
> *In apprehension, how like a god! The beauty of the world! The paragon of animals! And yet, to me, what is this quintessence of dust?*

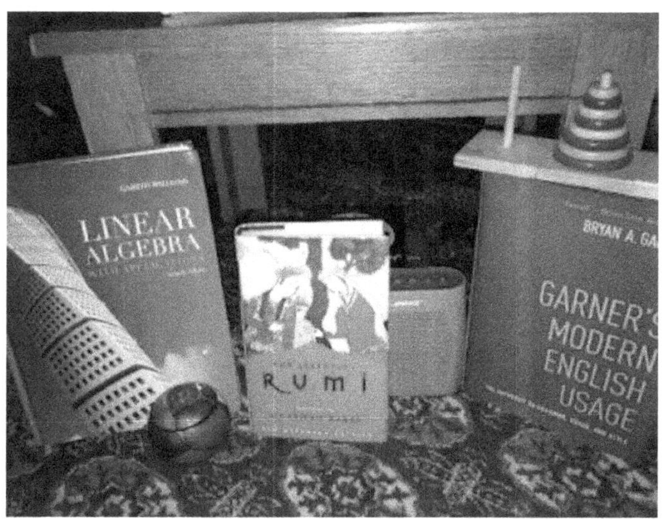

Postscript

As a postscript to the thread—this time drilling down to the level of the irreducible atoms that form the substrate of both code and prose—let's take a peek at the nexus between thought, words, prose, and code, the latter being the distillation of someone's attempt to reify the conceptualization of a process. And for that, I can scarcely do better than point you to writing maestro Donnel B. Stern who, in his trademark crystal-clear formulations, observes in his book, *Unformulated Experience* (Routledge), how Merleau-Ponty distinguishes *"empirical speech,"* that being the established usage of conventional expressions, from *"creative speech,"* which *"frees the meaning captive in the thing."*

Riveting Stuff

This is precisely the sort of riveting prose that knocks my socks off on a regular basis; the inseparable entanglement with the irreducible atoms which are the bedrock of code and prose; and another reason—perhaps, *the* reason—why designing and crafting (1) software code and (2) prose are inextricably woven into a unified tapestry which, at its finest, drives many of us in such pursuits. Put another way: Keep it direct, unadorned, simple, and elegant.

And this is *precisely* what the brilliant English novelist, essayist, and journalist George Orwell had in mind when he alerted us in his prescient essay *Politics and the English Language*, using a justifiably admonitory tone, how

> *As I have tried to show, modern writing at its worst does not consist in picking out words for the sake of their meaning and inventing images in order to make the meaning clearer. It consists in gumming together long strips of words which have already been set in order by someone else, and making the results presentable by sheer humbug.*

I used the phrase *"riveting prose"* above, and it relentlessly ushers in a flood of memories, this being a phrase which I first came across in the pages of a stellar book that has had, by far, the greatest impact on my writing: *Writing with Style: Conversations on the Art of Writing*, by John Trimble. If memory serves me right, I had remarked elsewhere how

When Graham's Hackers & Painters came out, many years ago (it predates my reading any of his works on Lisp), I was so impressed by its quality that I wrote to him, telling him how highly I thought of his book, plus recommending to him the best book available on this planet on writing well, namely Writing with Style: Conversations on the Art of Writing by John R. Trimble. Graham graciously replied to me, saying that, in fact, he, too, had a copy of Writing with Style in his bookshelf. I was pleasantly surprised because, while most everyone has heard of The Elements of Style (by Strunk and White), hardly anyone is aware of John R. Trimble's stellar gem of a book.

To my mind at least, and with all due respect to the former book—yes, I have read and appreciated its advice, too—*Writing with Style* is the book that *The Elements of Style* wants to be when it grows up.

The Takeaway

If you take away from this letter only one book to master in your writing journey, make it *Writing with Style: Conversations on the Art of Writing* by John R. Trimble. I refer to the volume fondly as *WWS*. My writing life can be cleanly divided—much as the World Wars (WW) divided history into pre- and post-WW—into pre- and post-*WWS*. There, I said that.

And yes, I got smitten by the pixie-dust magic qualities of em-dashes, which I alluded to earlier, directly as a result of reading Professor Trimble's classic and ever-sparkling *WWW*.

While on the subject, allow me to share merely a single excerpt, and a single sentence at that, from the works of one of the most elegant and precise writers of the world, the British mathematician and philosopher Bertrand Russell. As I share this, I can't help but pause and reflect on the current state of our world, and the irony of it all as Russell looked to *"men who were deeply imbued with a respect for law"*. He noted, in "Individual and Social Ethics" in *The Basic Writings of Bertrand Russell* (1961), how

> *It is noteworthy that the most successful revolutions— that of England in 1688 and that of America in 1776— were carried out by men who were deeply imbued with a respect for law.*

Prose doesn't get any more elegant, refined, and poignant than that, does it? And to really, *really* get those lovely interlopers— the em-dashes—out of my system, I'm going to do an ode for the road. Whether it bodes well or not, here goes...

An Ode To The Em-Dash

> *Yo, first things first, okay, strap yourself for a wild ride;*
> *I don't want anyone getting a Corvette whiplash*
> *You know the sort of thing that happens to rubber-neck-*
> *ers;*
> *Who blithely enjoy the scenery (while driving) until their*
> *car doth crash*
>
> *So you ask me, Where, oh where can we spot it?;*
> *You know, spot that magical, wee pixie em-dash!*
> *I'm so glad that you asked, and surely I was coming to that;*
> *What?! No, no, no: Keep the faith 'cuz this ain't no balder-*
> *dash*
>
> *Remember, good things come to those who wait;*
> *Things left behind by those who hustle like a thunder-*
> *flash*
> *Anyhow, should you ever feel that your writing is losing*

luster;
Don't fear; I will help you restore its glory with self-styled
panache

So don't you worry, and don't you cry;
And for heaven's sake, sheesh, please don't look so abash!
All you have to do is sprinkle some of that fabulous pixie-
dust;
On your writing and it will—it must—magically trans-
form ala the em-dash

But whatever you do, should you even wear a dental re-
tainer or two;
Do not—I repeat—do not grind your teeth in an angst-rid-
den gnash
For one, it would not be a pretty sight, and you might;
Even be accused of doing a monster-mash

Yo, much-maligned and grossly-underused punctuation
mark that it is;
We'll liberally use the em-dash without so much as batting
an eyelash
Lusterless writing begone, I say, weeds begone;
The em-dash is poised to dispel all that mishmash

No more comma-clogged sentences, no Sir, and no
Madam!;
And my name ain't Adam, it's Akram, and now we're done
with that news-flash
Clarity be thine nature, O writing, sweet as honey;
Unwittingly inebriated by a serendipitous nectar-splash

Get our of here, you tell me, to avoid a gash or two;
Hey, easy now, I'm outta here in a flash
Mark my words, though, to thine own em-dash be true;
For, should you not—wedged like so—we might come gate-

crash
Ow, ow, that'll teach you a lesson;
Darn, some people can be oh-so brash.
- Akram Ahmad (presenting, in its entirety, "An Ode To
The Em-dash")

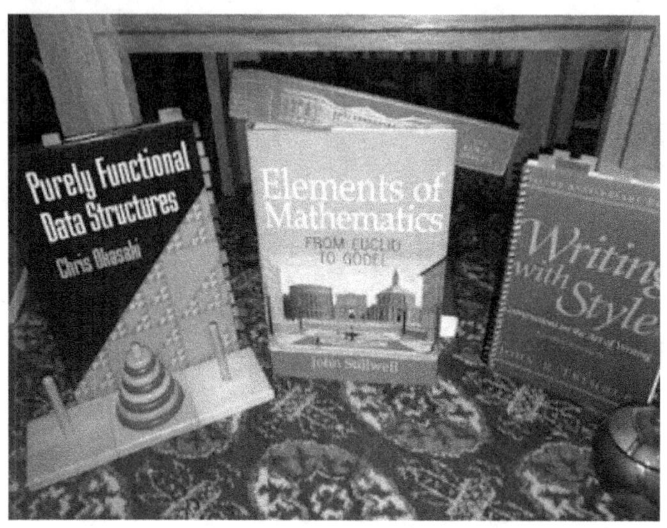

That Book With The Burgundy Cover

Some books fall into disuse; others into use; and *yet* others into overuse. My copy of this particular book—burgundy color and all—finds itself valiantly propped up against a table leg as in the picture above.

So my well-worn (paperback) copy of *Writing with Style: Conversations on the Art of Writing*, literally fell apart at the seams from, shall we say, extended use; the careful reader will note the spiral-bound copy toward the right-hand side in the pic.

Hackers Of The World (The Good Kind)

So I got to thinking about something that the noted Lisp hacker —and founder of *Y Combinator*, now the preeminent startup-company accelerator—Paul Graham had to say in connection with the pursuit of beauty in design. So I dug up my well-worn copy of *Hackers & Painters* (O'Reilly Media), harking back to my days in wintry Minnesota and boy, *was* I surprised, pleasantly so, I hasten to add, to rediscover, in revisiting its pages, just how profound and lasting an impact the pursuit of beauty has in creating and evolving designs of the highest order.

To give you a better flavor of Graham's take on this subtle matter, I really can't do much better than share some excerpts as I flip through the well-worn (*wizened*? although using this latter word would be a tad too anthropomorphic) pages of *Hackers & Painters*...

But first, some clarification of the term *hacker*—in the sense that in which it's used here—is in order:

> *A hacker is any skilled computer expert that uses their technical knowledge to overcome a problem...*

With that slight digression—merely a definitional one—out of the way, let's pause, catch our breath, and reflect on what it might mean to pursue beauty in the quest for creating and evolving software designs of the highest order.

More Than A Sylph Of A Link?

Yes, there seem to exist *more* than mere tenuous links between beauty and great software and prose. Come to think of it, the notion of beauty as a guiding principle to crafting great software —and prose, to be sure—has spawned an entire series of books on the pragmatic unity of beauty and technology, brought to us by the publishing industry's vanguard company we all fondly know as OReilly. The basis of the theme is nicely articulated by the editors (Diomidis Spinellis and Georgios Gousios) of the book *Beautiful Architecture* (O'Reilly), and I encourage you to check it out.

Finally, in wrapping up our exploration of how beauty can serve as an unerring guiding principle to crafting great software, glancing as we did at some ideas captured in the series of books on the pragmatically unifying approach of pursuing beauty in mastering technology, I also encourage you to check out what the editors (*viz* Andy Oram and John Viega) of yet another book in this series have to say on this subject.

There you have it, observations from the trenches of the software industry on exercising the imagination in the quest for beautiful unifying themes, weaving many strands into a unified and beautiful whole; truly, then, the whole is other than the sum of the parts.

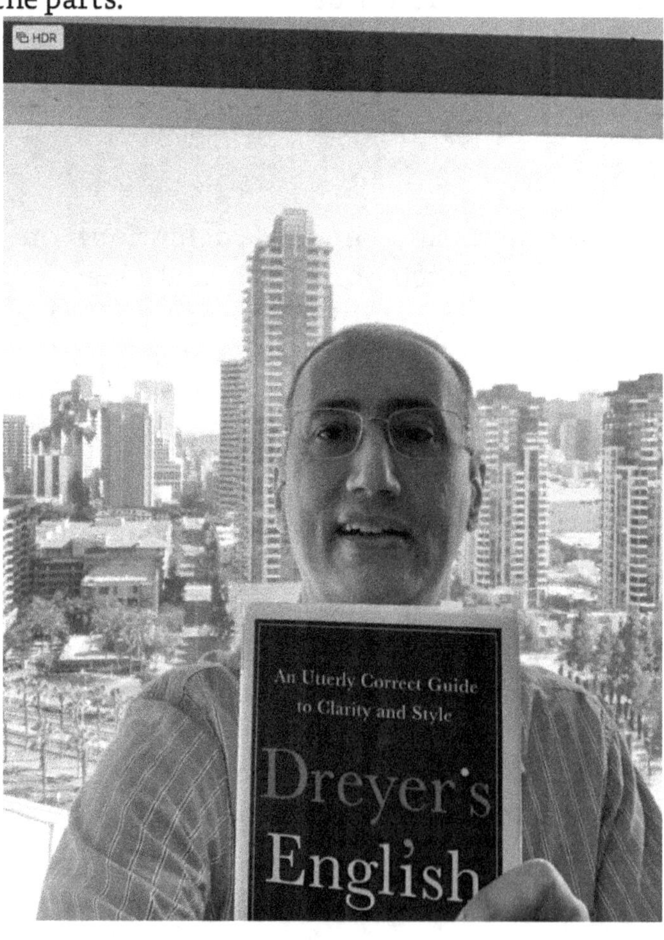

Dryer's Gem Pops Up...

...and rest assured that there will be more—*much* more—on the utter loveliness of the book that is *Dryer's English: An Utterly Correct Guide to Clarity and Style* (Random House) in the future. Chalk that up as a memo.

Meanwhile, we haven't even talked about beauty in the realm of those who pursue the endless frontier of Artificial Intelligence (aka AI.) Perhaps we can delve into that in a future essay. Let's settle at this time with a nod to Ray Kurzweil's nice book *How to Create a Mind: The Secret of Human Thought Revealed* (Penguin Group, US), in which he harks back to an earlier generation in asking about Wittgenstein's thoughts on issues such as beauty and love, all the while recognizing the inherent imperfections attendant on ideas as they swirl around in the minds of men—*and* women, to be sure.

On Intentionality

To that musing—and it happens to be a rather precise description of the magic and beauty of interpretations and reinterpretations—I can only add some poetic leavening by way of the words of celebrated American poet Robert Frost when he remarked how

> *I have never started a poem yet whose end I knew. Writing a poem is discovering.*

In sum, this letter—entitled *Beautiful Code, Beautiful Prose* as it is—could just as well have been entitled *Beautiful Prose, Beautiful Code.* Is this juxtaposition mere semantic hair-splitting, or are we on to something more profound? Which comes first, the code or the prose? But as I hope I've been able to demonstrate in this essay, the two are intimately bonded to each other—like unborn twins clasped in a fraternal hug—that we *might* as well embrace the ineluctable conclusion that any attempt to disentangle the two (the code from the prose), would be a futile exercise at best, and folly at worst.

And to bring closure to the metaphor of symbiosis, no book in my mind exemplifies this theme better than *Refactoring to Patterns* by Joshua Kerievsky (Addison-Wesley Professional). Noted software designer Ward Cunningham had remarked about this book that "*Now the connection between software patterns and agile development is finally told*".

It's That Little Bird Again...

A little blue bird tells me that it's time to wrap up. Plus, I have this sinking feeling that I've got way more material (on this subject) than can be covered in a single letter. So if anyone is interested, by all means let me know—either by replying with a letter of your own or by whispering in the ears of the little blue bird doing double duty as messenger pigeon—and your truly will get started on a future installment to elaborate on, and

delve into, any thematic aspects that grab your fancy. Deal?
With that, I invite you to use your powers of imagination to summon the serenity which dwells in the celebrated *Fallingwater* architecture, Frank Lloyd Wright's masterpiece, suspended as it is in glorious harmony with the surrounding foliage.

POSTSCRIPT

Having called the exchange of our eight letters a wrap, there still remains the matter of the curiosity that is the "postscript." Tacked on to the end of a letter—in this case to the end of a bunch of letters—a postscript has typically been used to rally final thoughts on the verge of getting lost to posterity.

But fear not, this postscript is here to give the glad tidings that, slowly but surely—one letter at a time—we are reviving the fine art of letter-writing, even as we navigate our lives through a frenzied world.

With that, shall we rally a handful of final thoughts lest they slip away into the sands of time?

Looking Past Superficial Similarities

Beautifully wrought prose, many will agree, singularly wields the power to make one's heart skip a beat. And elegantly crafted code has been known to make a heart sing. So why had nobody looked at these seemingly unrelated phenomena as a unified whole? We can, as I have sought to demonstrated in this book, divergent thinking-style, look *past* the superficial similarities between the endeavor each of crafting prose and that of designing code—writers rewrite their prose while programmers refactor their code, both work with abstractions, neither is immune to the occasional blockage of creative flow, which manifests itself in the writer's block and in the coder's jam, respectively, and so on. That's quotidian stuff.

We Need To Go Deeper

But deeper forces are at play, I believe, forces which inform their respective practice: How best to tease those forces out into revealing themselves so we can witness them in their glory?

Entered this book. Written as a series of letters to the practitioner, it aimed at connecting the dots between the ins and outs of crafting prose and those of designing code—tying the two together with the proverbial marriage knot—by delving deep into the interplay between the two. No longer would we have to scratch our head, wondering why nobody took on this vital interplay sooner.

With this book, I have done my best to take on nothing less than a rejuvenation of the craft by drawing on my experience of two decades as (1) a devoted software practitioner, and as (2) an inveterate writer. (It so happens that I'm the impresario of the immensely popular blog for geeks and non-geeks alike: ProgrammingDigressions.)

Where We Went

Among the many reflections which await you in the pages of this book: Can a practitioner care as much about the craft of prose as about designing code? Is one born with the skill of writing well, or can it be cultivated? More fundamentally, how best to learn things deeply and to their core? Where will our insatiable thirst for collecting idioms lead us? Does it make sense to diversify? More pointedly, how best to engage both our left brain (*think the analytical and the logical*) and the right brain (*think the creative and the inspired*) in our daily work?

This Is Your Book

This book is for geeks and non-geeks alike. Coming on the heels of the two acclaimed books—*"Dispatches from the Software Trenches"* and *"Postcards From The Software Island"*—in *The Programming Imagination* series, this book is for anyone who believes that playfulness is decidedly underrated, that life is positively not a zero-sum game, and it's especially for those who seek to rejuvenate the craft itself. Hence, the subtitle, "Essays on Rejuvenating the Craft."

Clear As Mud?

Oh, so I (myself a non-native speaker and lover of the English language) wish to make it abundantly clear that I do not consider myself a modern-day Joseph Conrad (who just happened to be *another* non-native speaker of the English language.) Far from it, though I candidly profess to have taken inspiration from at least some of the prose passages by said Polish writer, one who is regarded as one of the greatest novelists in the English language, and one who—relevantly enough to the ethos of this book—famously remarked how

> *My task, which I am trying to achieve is, by the power of the written word, to make you hear, to make you feel—it is, before all, to make you see.*

Wow! Talk about a lofty ideal. And if the book you hold took you a modest *halfway* to that ideal, I will chalk this up as "job accomplished."

❖ ❖ ❖

LETTERS FROM YOU

The story would be incomplete—to be precise, it would be half-complete—without the inclusion of the letters you have sent me, and of which there are thousands, I'm delighted to note. I picked a teensy handful, the ones which follow, to show my appreciation and round out the story:

kittyfassett
JULY 30, 2019 AT 6:57 PM

Akram, you are a true genius, breathing new life into my favorite writers in this brave new world that seems to remain forever beyond my grasp.

Christopher Diaz
OCTOBER 27, 2017 AT 1:16 PM

Your passion and dedication towards writing clearly shows in the thoughtful responses you provide. Lots of insightful posts, and I've barely scratched the surface!

Saqib Qazi
AUGUST 26, 2017 AT 8:15 AM EDIT

Dear Akram, I am entranced by the spirituality you have injected into your writing – its going to take me a few readings to absorb all the nuances!

Xin
JANUARY 18, 2021 AT 6:18 PM

Good point! Visualization does help memes to be spread. That might explain a lot of memes are quickly spread out through Instagram and YouTube nowadays. Good influencers know what images match with their contents.

Edward A. Lee
JUNE 25, 2019 AT 2:07 PM

Love it! Erudite and entertaining…

BeverlyMundyWeable
AUGUST 29, 2017 AT 4:25 PM

From sparkly em-dashes to Frank Lloyd Wright's masterpiece Fallingwater–I was challenged and intrigued and educated throughout. Thank you for pulling together so many sources to back up your insights. The English teacher part of me wants to weep with joy while the Business Systems Analyst side of me wonders, "Where in the world did he get the time, energy, and brain power to construct such an essay?"

‹ Previous

Best Scala Books

Next ›

Best Clojure Books

307 comments

« Older Comments

priya
JULY 31, 2020 AT 9:14 AM

Very interesting to read this article.I would like to thank you for the efforts you had made for writing this awesome article. This article inspired me to read more. keep it up.

Amey Shukla
MARCH 1, 2018 AT 8:13 AM

Hello. Thank you for the reply. I was a bit busy with exams so couldn't check. Me and some of my friends are absolutely loving your essays. Thanks for the great content.

Anonymous
JUNE 3, 2019 AT 3:04 PM

I'd like to thank you for the efforts you have put in writing this blog. I am hoping to check out the same high-grade blog posts by you in the future as well.

In truth, your creative writing abilities has motivated me to get my own, personal website now 😊

‹ Previous   Next ›

Eventual Consistency can be a Good Thing   Best Algorithms Books (Part 2)

196 comments

« Older Comments

Anonymous
MAY 15, 2019 AT 6:37 PM

It's hard to come by well-informed people on this topic, but you sound like you know what you're talking about!
Thanks

4 comments

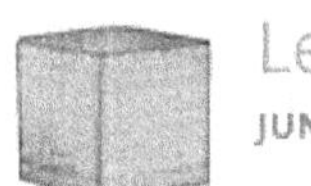

Lex Sheehan
JUNE 24, 2019 AT 2:46 PM

For us programmers, there is nothing like it on the planet. Where else can we go to be delightfully entertained and informed in prose? 🚀🚀🚀

Anonymous
JUNE 6, 2019 AT 12:47 PM

Can I simply just say what a comfort to uncover someone that genuinely understands what they're discussing over
the internet. You definitely understand how to bring
an issue to light and make it important. More and more people ought to look at this and understand this side of the story. I was surprised that you're not more popular given that you most certainly possess the gift.

Toby Mosby
NOVEMBER 19, 2018 AT 5:31 PM

Bravo Akram – lang may yer lum reek!

It was great to meet you and share in this experience on the edge in Ediburgh.

"Microservices, to be sure, have emerged from the molten-pit kindled by flames of a brave new world,..."

Love it!!

Lex Sheehan

NOVEMBER 1, 2018 AT 6:45 PM

Well done, Sir Akram!

I looked up "deid" and was not surprised to find that it was a Scottish form of the word "dead".

Your poem is at once insightful and colloquial to your travels, along with links to some of other articles; all of which blow my mind wide open.

These are no wee bonnie thoughts you share,
Nay!
They're rife with meaning and crafted with utmost care!

Thanks, again, for yet another piece of computer science artwork.

Best, Lex

M. Hunter

NOVEMBER 5, 2019 AT 2:08 AM

Akram, a wonderful 'digression' as always! Certainly, you make a good argument, hacking + anything requires one to be a bit of a coding contortionist.

There beyond (or before) what we classify as memory exist: natural instincts, a first kiss, and the way our hearts beat without us even having to ask.

I've always found the ability to create new things, for instance on (or with) a computer, super-fantastic! Let us take this moment to thank our thumbs for remembering which is right and which is left.

Thank you for reminding us that we can enjoy Archimedean solids, and logic gates, and dogs playing poker; if not always simultaneously... =D

◆ ◆ ◆

TESTIMONIALS

I nearly left this section out—we geeks tend to shy away from talking about ourselves, don't we?

So yeah, the only reason I *did* decide to retain this section is to level-set, because chances are that you haven't heard of me: Sort of to help you get to know me a bit better (and where my ideas and I come from. "*Go to the source,*" as the adage would have it, amirite?)

With that, here are some blurbs—and here I headed over to my LinkedIn profile to grab a handful of testimonials—ones that you just *might* find interesting. (Should you start to tire, *please* feel free to sail right past this stuff, and jump into the book proper.)

One more time, we're just breaking the ice at this point...

kitty fassett
retired pianist
December 9, 2017, kitty and
Akram were students together

As a brilliant translator and supremely gifted writer, Akram Ahmad draws inspiration from a prodigious knowledge of a world of great literature and poetry. His blogs, decorated always with the perfect choice of artwork, flow with charm and originality and are a feast for the eyes and a joy to read.

Edward Lee
Robert S. Pepper
Distinguished Professor,
EECS Department, UC
Berkeley
June 22, 2018, Edward was
Akram's mentor

Akram is a true artist who deftly practices the art and craft of writing. He has a deep insight into software technologies and writes about them with humor, poetry, and well-chosen illustrations. His blog is a delight to read. I recommend him highly!

Ger Hallissey
Senior Manager –
Advanced Research, Office
of the Products and
Operations CTO at Dell
Technologies
March 4, 2021, Ger worked
with Akram in different groups

I had the pleasure of participating in the OCTO Book Club that Akram chaired during his time at Dell Technologies. Akram led the discussions, encouraging active participation from all. He diligently captured, eloquently summarized and faithfully distributed key insights and learnings from each meeting. Akram is passionate about technology, a committed life-long learner, a gifted conversationalist and writer, and a great person to have on your team. **See less**

Eric Cotter
Technical Staff | Office of
the CTO "research group"
at Dell EMC
September 17, 2020, Akram
worked with Eric in the same
group

Akram is one of those amazing gems you find as you move your way through life.
I have been truly inspired by his intellect, insights, and technical prowess. His exceptional attention to detail always impresses me. On numerous occasions he has brought to my attention "new ideas" or new ways of doing something. He conducts his daily work with a zest for life and love for his trade. I unabashedly wholeheartedly support Akram in his career moving forward and could not recommend him more highly. I have had the distinct privilege of working with Akram over these last 2 years. Some people go the extra mile, Akram goes the extra parsec. His education and experience shine through in his communication with our customers and his co-workers. Akram's demonstrable talents in Go, Java, Docker, Kubernetes and system design and deployment have been on display over these last two years. Bravo Akram!
See less

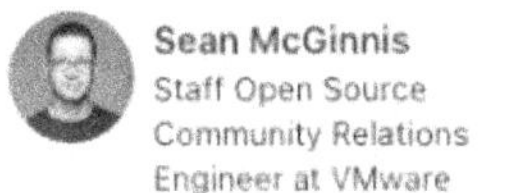**Sean McGinnis**
Staff Open Source
Community Relations
Engineer at VMware

September 23, 2020, Sean
worked with Akram in different
groups

Akram is always an energetic and insightful person to speak to. Whether organizing a book club to foster thoughtful creativity across the Office of the CTO, or talking through deep technical concepts, Akram has always been excited and engaged, thinking through ideas and what impact they may have in other areas of our work.

Akram has a broad set of technical skills, whether it is programming in Python, Go, or Java, or architecting overall system design for Edge or containerization with Kubernetes.

He is always willing to speak up and share ideas. Working with researchers and academia, he brought multiple insights to the group for ways to be a more effective distributed team. He has always been great at being able to apply insights from different problem domains to the problem at hand.

Akram has a great skillset, being able to take broad and abstract ideas, and use his solid technical skills to bring those ideas to life. <u>See less</u>

Okay, that'll do for now. (In all seriousness, though, I am *oh-so* humbled by these—and other—testimonials I've received over the years. I *truly* am, straight up from the heart.)
And hey, it was so nice to meet you (yet again), dear Reader.

AFTERWORD

They have been at a great feast of languages, and stol'n the scraps.
- Moth: [Aside to Costard] (in William Shakespeare's King Lear)

Though we may have come to an end, let's seize this moment as a beginning instead....

Our idyll—and along with it the charmed correspondence between us two—has drawn to a close. Why, though, should parting be such sweet sorrow?

(Speaking of that Shakespearean allusion about the theme of us parting ways, I can't help but glance further up—check Moth's aside to Costard—and note that the *"great feast of languages"* I had in mind was all about the joy of playing with language, or *languages* really, in the plural, since we bounced back-and-forth, trampoline-style, during the course of our letters. If I've helped you glean a bit more than *"stol'n scraps,"* I'll chalk this book up as having accomplished its mission.)

To come full circle—especially with my having begun the *Afterword* on the admittedly lachrymose note of us parting ways—I am going out on a limb to assert that some *celebration* is called for. Here's why.

Dare I say that we—*you* and I, respectively the *reader* and writer—have managed to pull off nothing less than a *revival* of the fine art of letter-writing in a world besotted with the quick thrills of texting and other social media? I claim that what we have accomplished in these pages counts for something. We slowed down to speed up: Why is everyone in a mad rush anyway? I say so ruefully because, based on the minor research that I've conducted, one simply *has* to slow down to speed up; *"stay steady, stay smart,"* is another way to put it.

And don't you even get me started on what a refusal—worse still, an outright denial—of the wisdom inherent in that popular phrase (i.e. *"stay steady, stay smart*) may bode for us a species (of the *homo sapiens* kind.)

That, dear Reader, would take me a whole nother book to explain...

Maybe you *do* want to read more stuff like this—and I might decide to *write* some more—so why don't we keep this dialog going?

(I'm positively not psychic, so please be sure to let me know if you're interested in reading more stuff like the one is this book.)

I'm eminently approachable. In fact, I *invite* contact. (Check the *"My Coordinates"* section just around the corner.) Be in touch.

Till we chat next, I bid you farewell. (I hope my letters meant something to you; they sure did—*and* do—to me.)

MY COORDINATES

Be in touch. My coordinates, once again, are as follows. Much as I said earlier, I invite contact—via any and all of these:

Blog → Programming Digressions: Essays
LinkedIn → This is a good way to stay in touch with me
Twitter → I occasionally do tweet
Github: My open source contributions
Email → It's there, *should* you wish...

◆ ◆ ◆

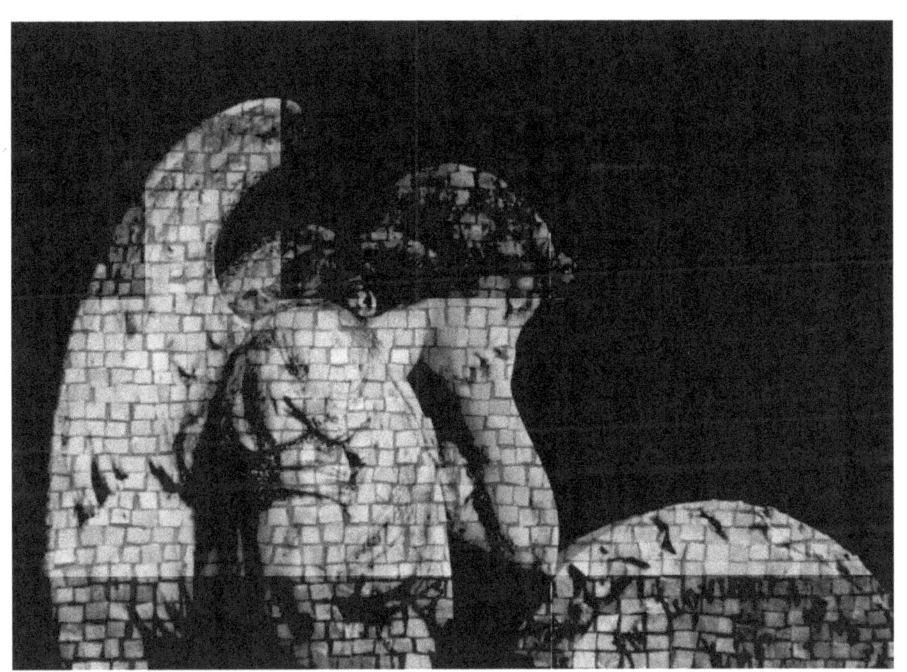